Sales and Sales Management in Financial Services

A Hands-on Guide to Global Best Practices

By Sandy Vaci

Book 1 in the Keys to Sales Success series

Searching finance

First published 2011 by Searching Finance Ltd, 8 Whitehall Road, London W7 2JE, UK

ISBN: 978-1-907720-03-1

Typeset by Deirdré Gyenes

Cover image by iStockphoto

Sales and Sales Management in Financial Services

A Hands-on Guide to Global Best Practices

By Sandy Vaci

Book 1 in the Keys to Sales Success series

Searching finance

About the author

Sandy Vaci is an international bank executive with 30 years' experience across four continents, in close to 50 countries. He has held executive positions at companies such as Citibank's Global Consumer Bank, Procter & Gamble, the Royal Bank of Scotland Group, Raiffeisen International and the Canadian Imperial Bank of Commerce.

He is currently Senior Lecturer in Marketing and Sales at the Maastricht School of Management and the Business School of Central European University. He is also Chairman of the Supervisory Board of the Credit Bank of Moscow and advises a wide range of companies on global best practices. His client list includes Barclays Bank, UniCredit Group, Eureko Insurance, Unilever, and the National Commercial Bank of Jamaica.

As a true 'global citizen', Sandy has three home bases (Toronto, Vienna, Budapest) which he shares with his wife of 25 years, Judit.

Acknowledgements

The author wishes to thank the following people for their support:

Mr David Straker, ChangingMinds.org (UK). For kind permission to use the material on sales closing techniques from his www.ChangingMinds.org website.

Ms Ann Tierney, director, Searching Finance Ltd (UK). For suggesting this book in the first place and for helping to make it reality.

Dr Judit Acs, partner, 3-i Inc. Strategic Consultancy (Canada). For her help, support and quality control of the work.

About Searching Finance Ltd

Searching Finance Ltd is a dynamic new voice in knowledge provision for the financial services and related professional sectors. Our mission is to provide expert, highly relevant and actionable information and analysis, written by professionals, for professionals. For more information, please visit www.searchingfinance.com

Also available from Searching Finance Ltd

There are two companion volumes in the 'Keys to Sales Success' series for financial sales practitioners. 'Channel Innovation in Financial Services: A Practitioner's Guide to Development and Integration' looks at non-branch channels – franchise and agent set-ups, mobile bankers, phone banking, social media and issues around channel integration. 'Segmentation and Marketing in Financial Services: Best Practices from CRM to FMCG' examines current marketing practices and how they support the sales process.

CONTENTS

List of Tables

List of Figures

Abbreviations

AC	Acquisition Cost – direct cost of acquiring a new customer or account
ACCT	Account – such as deposit, current, revolving credit accounts
ATM	Automated Teller Machine, sometimes also called ABM (Automated Banking Machine)
ATL	Above The Line marketing, e.g. advertising, PR, sponsorships, internet
BAU	Business As Usual – the level of (new) business that should be expected without proactive actions or extenuating factors (sometimes also called 'walk-in', in the case of branches)
BDR	Business Development Representative
BEP	Branch Efficiency Project
BTL	Below The Line marketing, e.g. direct mail and outbound sales calls
C/A	Current Account / Checking Account – transactional, 'household' account
CAPEX	Capital Expenditures – upfront spending for capital goods acquisition or improvements (e.g. when setting up a branch)
CC	Credit Card
CIR	Cost-to-Income-Ratio
CRM	Customer Relationship Management (sometimes, but *not* in this study, also referring to Credit Risk Management)
DIY	Do-It-Yourself, home renovation retail stores
FTE	Full Time Equivalent person – one additional headcount, assuming full time work by it, at 100%
FTL	Fixed Term Loan
GDP	Gross Domestic Product – the total local output of a country's economy
HNWI	High Net Worth Individual(s) – people with potential or worth above core customers but below private banking prospects or clients
IT	Information Technology – refers both to the department that handles software / hardware support and to the software / hardware set up itself
IVR	Interactive Voice Response system – automated call response software, usually used in call centres
JV	Joint Venture – a company set up by two or more separate entities owing it, setting direction, benefiting from gains and bearing losses together

KPI	Key Performance Indicators – essential measures to track how the business is doing on an ongoing basis
L/C	Line of Credit – revolving line, can be drawn on at will
M&A	Mergers and Acquisitions – usually refers to acquiring another business, not to being acquired
NIM	Net Interest Margin – the (average) difference between the interest rate paid on deposits and the rate charged on loans; the margin a bank makes
NPV	Net Present Value – the aggregated current value of something that may take a long time to generate returns (it accounts for the cost of the money, so current returns are more highly valued that returns later on)
NSF	No Sufficient Funds – when there are not enough funds in an account to cover payments initiated from that account by the customer
O/D	Overdraft – a line of credit attached to an account, usually a current account
PI	Private Individual segment within retail banking customers (the other main segment being SME)
P&L	Profit and Loss (responsibility) – bottom line (accountability)
POS	Point-of-Sale, for banks it also refers to 'sales finance' or 'consumer finance' – granting credit to customers at retail outlets to allow purchase of goods (or, rarely, services)
PR	Public Relations – managing a company's image with the public, without advertising or promotional means
REA	Real Estate Agent
ROA	Return On Assets
ROE	Return On Equity
S/A	Savings Account
SBU	Strategic Business Unit – usually a business unit with its own objectives, authorities and P/L responsibility
SFA	Sales Force Automation (software) – part of a CRM set up
SLA	Service Level Agreement – pre-agreed level of service deliverables between departments or units of the same company
SME	Small and Medium-sized Enterprise – small businesses
SMS	Short Messaging System – sending text messages through mobile phones
SW	Software
SWOT	Strengths, Weaknesses, Opportunities and Threats – a way to evaluate a business based on internal and external factors
TD	Term Deposit, also called Certificate of Deposit (CD), Guaranteed Investment Certificate (GIC), etc.

TOC Take on Cost – the cost of acquiring a new account, expressing the acquisition cost as a percentage of the average balance acquired with the account. Useful for fixed term, fixed balance sales, such as personal loans or fixed term deposits

TQM Total Quality Management – service quality initiatives that cover the whole company

T/L Term Loan, to be repaid over a set period of time, in instalments

U&A Usage and Attitude study – research to understand how consumers use products and how they relate to them (what expectations they have)

USP Unique Selling Proposition – the kind of benefits and features that make our offer uniquely better (different) from the competition's

VIP Very Important Person – high value customer or prospect, also referred to as 'Premium Segment'

Introduction

Thank you for picking up this book – whether electronically, or in paper form. If you have already bought it – congratulations! I hope you will enjoy it. If not yet, let me tell you what you can expect from it.

Why this book?

I wrote it because I felt practitioners in financial services were missing a *practical* guide to sales in their field. Sure, there are a number of books that talk about one narrow area such as 'engagement-based selling' or 'call centre processes'. There are also quite a few 'strategic guides' and books on the latest management fads.
But what is missing is something that summarises all the key elements of selling and sales management in financial services and provides practical examples, benchmarks and implementation templates for them. That is the book that you are now looking at.

Why is it different?

I wrote it based on my 30 years in the business and tried to pack it full of practical tips I learned along the way. Who cares about the strategic importance of selecting the best branch location if you don't know how to do it in practice? What are the specific rules of cross-selling – what, to whom, when and why? How should you set up your organisation cross-border? How should you manage your sales team on a daily basis by leading indicators, to guarantee success? It's questions like these I wanted to answer for you.

I believe that:

- Branches should not be discarded or redesigned to be something other than a branch. They should be kept, improved, built on, added to, innovated on and integrated better;
- Longitudinal integration is needed along sales management and sales process lines to ensure upfront plans are followed through with high efficiency activities;
- Cross-functional and cross-channel integration should be a way of life – training, marketing, reward systems and other elements need to work together in a harmonious way;
- Many studies on the topic of sales and business efficiencies have not taken the required holistic approach to really help the general practitioner. Too high level, too narrowly focused, strategic only, or only executionally oriented guides are not very efficient themselves;
- One needs to start with the branches and general sales management / sales process disciplines. All elements of sales efficiency-related items (from location selection to training modules to best ways of cross-selling – and beyond) need to be reviewed and tied together. Innovative new approaches and 'glue elements' tying it all together need to be included later;
- Both strategic and executional elements should be reviewed. 'How to' and 'watch out for' guides, check lists and templates are needed. Only with a full coverage of all these items can one expect the reader to be able to put all the

elements learned from a study to profitable use. And, after all, that should be the purpose of any book such as this.

What does it have?

The book itself breaks into several parts. We first review branch set-ups and sales management components in detail. We spend time on frequently overlooked key issues such as capacity allocation and sales meeting schedules. We look at management fads such as insisting on profit targets for everyone – showing where they are wrong and what works instead. There are templates for everything, from training modules to physical location selections.

Next comes needs-based selling, including segmentation approaches to help define the needs to target. Tips on sales engagements and a list of more than 60 closing techniques are also reviewed. Global best practices are summarised next, with an interesting addition (I hope): an implementation guide for them that allows you to look at it as though you are a consultant to your own company!

We finish by looking at moving our sales practices cross-border, into new markets. What works, what doesn't, what are the different types of organisational set-ups we can use, how to address the many practical issues such a move presents.

How will it help me?

First, I hope it will give you a good grounding in the key components that make up 'sales' in financial services. Second, it should provide enough practical guidance and benchmarks so that you can implement all the best practices reviewed – and know how you are doing versus the competition. I also hope it will help you defend your common sense position on the right business practices in the face of management myths and consulting 'gurus'.

I hope you will enjoy and benefit from this survey of the many sales issues, strategies and their practical applications. If you have any comments, please contact either the publisher at enquiries@searchingfinance.com or me directly at sandyvaci@yahoo.com.

You can also contact me at the above email address if you need more in-depth help or support. That is what I do now. I help companies become the best, by helping them integrate global best practices into what they have – instead of advocating throwing away your current practices so that I can sell you something new...

If you feel there are things missing on channel set-ups and the latest in sales / service delivery, fear not. This book is the first of a three-volume series entitled 'Keys to Sales Success.' Book 2, 'Channel Innovation in Financial Services: A Practitioner's Guide to Development and Integration' reviews non-branch channels – franchise and agent set-ups, mobile bankers, phone banking, social media, issues around channel integration and more. Book 3, 'Segmentation and Marketing in Financial Services: Best Practices from CRM to FMCG' examines current marketing practices and how they support the sales process. Together, they form a complete hands-on guidance package for sales professionals.

Happy reading!

Chapter 1

Branches – an integrated approach to boost sales efficiencies

Industry experience over the past several years shows that branches are here to stay, in more or less the same format as they are today. Market research also tells us that branches are still the most used of all delivery channels. It is therefore imperative, before considering other channels or approaches to improve sales efficiencies, that one addresses the issue of improving sales efficiencies through traditional branches. This goes beyond simply redirecting the efforts sales staff from administrative duties to proactive selling.

In my experience only a fully integrated approach, addressing and connecting all elements of sales efficiency-related areas, will achieve noticeable results. It is also my belief that most financial institutions take a more narrowly focused, pragmatic, but less all-encompassing approach in addressing branch sales issues. As a result, lasting improvements are rare.

For example, sales training without increased expectations based on the training and without fitting the expected training results into an overall sales management / sales process framework will not deliver optimal results. Similarly, layering in proactive sales processes without ensuring that sales capacity is available to execute along the new lines will result in marginal improvements, at most. Not aligning acquisition target segments between credit risk management, marketing and sales will virtually ensure low customer catchment efficiencies.

An integrated approach to improving sales efficiencies through branches will address all the key components of efficiency drivers, in an integrated way:

- Branch location selection;
- Premises;
- Business area alignments;
- Integrated perspective and benchmarking of all sales components;
- Capacity planning;
- Training;
- Sales planning, objective setting;
- Sales management;
- Proactive and reactive sales processes;
- Tracking and reward systems;
- Other enablers such as marketing and IT support, operations, etc.

This chapter will review all the above elements, present templates for their application and discuss the results of two tests regarding an integrated branch sales boost approach.

Location selection

The two major questions any branch location selection approach must answer are:

1. Should we open / keep a branch in this general area?
2. If yes, where should we locate it?

The first can be answered based on macro criteria – general guidelines.
The second, based on micro criteria – local guidelines.

Location selection at both levels should be scorecard driven to ensure consistency. Scorecard criteria must be agreed upfront and should not be deviated from. Agreed elements of scorecards should include:

1. Types of criteria used;
2. How to assign score values for each criterion;
3. Weighting of score values to derive composite value;
4. Decisions driven by composite values (cut-off points).

Macro criteria

Macro criteria should include:

- Market potential –
  - Population base;
  - Catchment potential;
  - Size of target segment(s);
  - Value of prospect base per capita;
  - Income per capita (if 'value per capita' not available);
  - Current market share, other own branches in area;
- Competitive environment –
  - Presence of competition, scored on an 'opportunity / threat' scale;
- Internal financial feasibility –
  - Revenue expectations per staff (e.g. discounted cashflow needed);
  - Cost projected per staff (e.g. CAPEX needed).

Micro criteria

Micro criteria normally include:

- Security;
- Accessibility;
- Visibility;
- Traffic – volume and type, variability (seasonal, daily);

- Mass transit presence;
- Parking;
- Site size, availability and flexibility;
- Local development expectations;
- Contract issues, cost.

Macro scorecard

Each of the eight sub-components of the three major elements should have the following defined for it:

- Calculation / definition;
- Scoring criteria;
- Weighting criteria.

Note: It is either 'value of prospect base per capita' or 'income per capita', but not both, hence eight sub-categories, not the nine listed. Weighting of their values may differ, based on which one is used. If 'value per prospect' can be calculated, a higher weighting should be used than if only 'income per capita' is available.

Examples

Population base

- Defined as those living or working in town;
- Scores:
  - 1 if below 10,000;
  - 2 if 10,000 to 50,000;
  - 3 if 50,000 to 100,000;
  - 4 if 100,000 to 500,000;
  - 5 if above 500,000;
- Weight in total composite score at 20%.

Catchment potential

- Defined as the percentage of the population base that can be reached from a given location;
- Scores:
  - 1 if below 2%;
  - 2 if 2% to 5%;
  - 3 if 5% to 10%;
  - 4 if 10% to 20%;
  - 5 if above 20%;

- Weight in total composite score at 10%.

Size of target segment

- Defined as the percentage of the catchment potential base that falls within the bank's target for new customers;
- Scores:
    - 1 if below 5%;
    - 2 if 5% to 15%;
    - 3 if 15% to 35%;
    - 4 if 35% to 75%;
    - 5 if above 75%.
- Weight in total composite score at 10%.

Value of prospect base per capita / income per capita

- Either the revenue that can be expected to be made on each relationship sourced from the target segment, or the average income per capita in the area;
- Scores: depend on the bank's profit model and hurdle rates;
- Weight in total composite score at 20% (if revenue figure is available) to 10% (if only income numbers are available).

Current market share

- Defined as the percentage of the target segment the bank already has in the area, through its other branches or through other channels;
- Scores:
    - 1 if over 50%;
    - 2 if 50% to 25%;
    - 3 if 25% to 10%;
    - 4 if 10% to 5%;
    - 5 if less than 5%;
- Weight in total composite score at 10%.

Competition

To assign score value for the competitive environment one should do 'sub-scoring' first, to assess if competitive presence is an opportunity or a threat. Having weak competitors in an area may be an advantage because the bank can provide a better alternative. This could mean a ready supply of customers defecting from weaker competitors. However, the opposite is true with stronger competitors.

A way to assess competitors is to look at key elements of their presence, assign values to them and weigh them. For simplicity, the assigned values could be between -5 (when they are worse than our bank, hence an opportunity) and +5 (when they are better and, hence, a threat). Weighting factors could be between 4 and 1, based on the importance of each area. The suggested four key elements to be used to assess whether they are an opportunity to source customers from, or a threat to lose customers to, are:

1. Service level compared to us – better, same or worse. This is the most important factor, suggested weight: 4;
2. Positioning – level of overlap between their target segment and ours, their positioning to the market and ours. Suggested weight: 3;
3. Communication strength – how effectively they communicate, how strong their media presence and share of mind is. Suggested weight: 2;
4. Size – their resources, national distribution coverage, etc. Suggested weight: 1.

The above approach would give a score value between -20 and +20 for each competitor. Multiplying the score values by the number of their branches in our trade area, then totalling up these values provides an overall score for the competitive environment. This score is usually between +100 and -100, based on five competitive branches in a given trade area. The widest practical range experienced in the market should then be split into five bands and score values assigned to them. A score of 5 should be the best for us, corresponding with the lowest competitive band. A score of 1 should correspond to the highest competitive band.

The 1 to 5 score value assigned could then be weighted at 15% for the total composite score of the scorecard.

Revenue per staff

- Appropriate internal definition (yearly gross revenue, net revenue, discounted cashflow, other);
- Scores: depend on bank's profit model and hurdle rates;
- Weight in total composite score at 10%.

Expense per staff

- Appropriate internal definition (CAPEX, yearly total allocated costs, other);
- Scores: depend on the bank's profit model and hurdle rates;
- Weight in total composite score at 5%.

Comments

- Weighting in the total composite score can of course vary, based on each bank's objectives and strategies. However, the weightings described so far add up to about 70% for market potential, 15% for competitive factors and 15% for internal factors. This has been proven as a fairly good overall split, because market potential should be by far the most important factor in the overall decision of opening or closing a branch. Within the internal financial factors, it is also better to weight revenue more heavily than costs, since the latter depends more on strictly internal, controllable, factors.

- The total composite weightings should of course add up to 100%.
- Each location should be scored for each criterion, score values weighted and added up. The total composite score value should then drive open / close / review decisions. The maximum total weighted composite score value for the scorecard described here is 500.
- It is acceptable to have tolerance ranges around composite score values, of about 10% in each direction, where management may decide which way to swing the decision.
- Based on the above, for example, branch location decisions at the macro level could be as follows:
  - Total score of 300 and above – keep / open;
  - Total score of 200 to 300 – review;
  - Total score of 200 or less – close / do not open;
  - In each case a +/- 25 score difference can be overridden by management.

It is strongly suggested that the scorecard approach outlined in this section be templated in an easy to use Excel spread sheet or similar, using the logic presented. While a detailed description such as the one given here is useful, experience suggests only templated branch location scorecards are used with any frequency. It is simply too cumbersome to use manuals for this purpose.

Micro scorecard

A separate scorecard for local guidelines can also be developed. The simplest way is again to assign score values and weighting factors to each. However, local selection criteria are on the one hand more qualitative (e.g. assessing visibility) and on the other hand more cut and dried (e.g. contract and cost issues). As a result, local site selection usually has a higher level of personal input from qualified professionals and less of a 'template driven', quantitative (statistical) approach.

Premises

A lot has been written about branch layouts and design and most banks have their own 'model branch' guidelines already. That is therefore not the focus of this book. Premises will only be discussed as being an influencer of branch sales efficiency.

The following guidelines are recommended for an efficient model branch design:

1. The layout must be inviting, open, easy to walk into – Walk-in traffic is an important element of building the business and should not be discouraged. Similarly, the windows should allow a view into the interior. The premises should also be lit when the branch is closed. These are basic rules but often disregarded.

2. The overall design should be high quality but in a human way – It should not look too expensive. It should definitely not look too intimidating.
3. The layout and signage should clearly direct customers and prospects to the right area – A (potential) customer should never be allowed to line up twice by mistake, choosing the wrong area first. Many of them will rather walk out than line up again – a loss of potential business.
4. Meeter / greeter function should be part of the branch design if at all economically feasible (mid-to-larger size branches) – The objectives of this are to speed up processing customers and to ensure that any walk-in prospect is captured with high efficiency.
5. Areas should be clearly blocked off using different (but complementary looking) materials and internal design elements. Consideration for defining different areas include:

- *Type of transaction:*
  a. High speed self service transactions using ATMs or other self-serve terminals;
  b. Interactive transactions with tellers / cashiers, requiring highly efficient and convenient processes;
  c. More time-demanding consultative selling / servicing interactions, such as opening more complicated accounts, discussing needs;
  d. Involved discussions, for example discussing mortgage needs or investment portfolio set-ups.
- *Type of customer segment:*
  a. SME (small and medium-sized enterprise, 'small business') clients – They may need specially trained account managers. Their cash in/out activities can be very time-consuming, requiring drop-off boxes and special processes to handle counting the money during off hours. Their upfront sales sessions can be very involved, taking a long time;
  b. Premium customers – They may need a separate area for discussing their needs, with dedicated account managers.
- *Type of sales activity:*

  As discussed later in this chapter (see 'Capacity reallocation'), physical space needs to be separated out for those sales staff involved in proactive prospecting for parts of their time. A good model branch design takes this into account upfront.

6. Customer needs (e.g. fast cash transactions, privacy for sales consultations) should be taken into account. Similarly, customer needs should be researched whenever fundamental decisions on the branch design are considered. One example may be whether or not to introduce a 'take a number' system. Often, management will argue that such an approach denigrates the image of the bank, by bringing it closer to a post office outlet, for example. However, customers tend to like the approach if

handled right, because it ensures no accidental double lining up and has an element of basic fairness, that of 'first come, first served'. This may be especially important for elderly and well-to-do clients.

7. Processes must be part of the model branch design – It is not enough to have a pleasant, well-working layout. Sales and administrative processes should also be 'model branch-compliant' to ensure the efficient layout is matched by efficient processes, using it to full advantage.

8. 'Stick close to your knitting' – In other words, keep in mind that a bank branch, at the end of the day, should be just that – a bank branch. Not a coffee shop, not a kindergarten, not a travel agency; customers expect a branch. Studies show (e.g. 'Branch of the Future', by Novametrie) that more than three-quarters of consumers expect their ideal branch to closely resemble their current branch and not be of a radically different design.

Results to be expected

If site selection is done right, and other elements of sales management implemented properly, the goals shown in Table 1.1 should be achievable with new branches.

Table 1.1: Branch break-even and payback benchmarks

	Break-even	Payback
Private individual customers only	3–5 years	6–8 years
Mixed-branch, including SME	1–2 years	3–4 years

Source: 3-i Inc

Alignments

In order to be effective, the sales area and its activities need to be aligned with all other parts of the organisation and its goals and processes. Although this may sound trivial, it is nevertheless a key area of neglect in many organisations. This is usually not due to malicious intent, but simply to a lack of recognition of the many coordinating steps needed. This section should help with the key issues in this area.

Alignment must be in place on several fronts:

- Business objectives;
- Target segments;
- Overall annual department / division plans;
- Activity plans;
- Cross-functional sales processes;
- Cross-functional capacity planning.

Business objectives

Any and all sales plans must be in line with overall business objectives. Daily branch sales plans, in the end, need to add up to the specific yearly product sales and portfolio targets of the bank. The objectives of the different SBUs (strategic business units) – marketing, credit and financial control – must all be matching and complementary.

A very strong gatekeeping function is a must to keep the alignment going through the year. Any bank that does not have one, at an operating level (as opposed to executive level) will experience delays in implementing sales activities. It should be expected that different product areas will try to push their own interests, especially if they are falling short of plan or receive management encouragement to be more aggressive. Special 'sales boost' initiatives should also fit into the overall plans and not be scheduled on their own.

Cascading and sequential planning is needed. For example, credit cards are usually good acquisition offers. Personal loans may be cross-sold to credit card customers with enough extra debt servicing ability. Personal loans sales may not achieve objectives if credit card sales fall short of plan and thus do not provide enough cross-sell target customers. Interlocking sales objectives should be well understood by all and routinely reviewed throughout the year.

Target segments

Target segment definitions from a business, credit risk, marketing and sales delivery perspective should be matched. Only the overlapping area of target segments from these different perspectives offers real selling efficiencies.

Overall business objectives dictate overall product sales objectives, hence the basic target segment to target for proactive selling. However, it makes no sense to target any member of this first cut of the target segment with a credit product unless there is a good chance that the prospect will actually be approved for the credit product offered. Marketing activities should therefore be directed only at those who are expected to qualify for the credit offer. Note that this goes beyond pre-approved credit offers. Marketing target lists for credit products should always be agreed with credit risk management.

Additionally, only those of the credit-approved target segment who can actually obtain the product (easily) should be targeted. Therefore, sales coverage should be overlaid on the target list. In some cases, local vetting of direct marketing lists by branches may also make sense, especially if local follow-up is planned by branch staff. Net/net, the overlapping area of business, credit, marketing, sales / distribution-based target segments is the actual segment that should be targeted for real efficiency.

Overall annual department / division plans

The marketing department, specific SBUs (strategic business units with product sales accountabilities) and the sales department all have objectives to reach and plans to support those objectives. These need to be co-ordinated in terms of:

- Timing;
- Product focus;
- Spending;
- Allocation of effort;
- Channel focus;
- Target prospects / customers.

It should be noted that the 'target prospect / customer' reference here includes not only what has been described in the previous section (co-ordination of targeting from different perspectives, targeting the overlap area among segments for best results) but also the setting up of 'contact rules' to ensure highest impact of messages sent to different segments.

Contact rules need to be set both within individual areas (such as sales, marketing, etc) and overall. The rules may vary based on the target segment, product mix to sell, and more. For example, the sales process for SME prospects should allow for three contacts just to 'warm up' the prospect, before actual specific selling activity starts. With private individuals (PI) proactive sales should be attempted at the first contact. Therefore, it is acceptable to have a 'maximum five contacts per two-month period by the same sales person' with SME but not with PI prospects.

Obviously, the maximum number of contacts for sales activities (as opposed to mandatory communication, such as statements and notices) needs to be regulated overall. Therefore, marketing, sales and SBU plans need to be co-ordinated to ensure allowed contacts are allocated in the most efficient way.

Specific, one-off, sales efforts need to fit within the overall plan of the bank to ensure alignment. This leads to co-ordinating specific activity plans.

Activity plans

Any sales activity planned must fit into the overall activity plan of the bank. Tracking and rewarding should also be based on the results of (overlapping) activities. Products sold at the end are the result of:

- Central initiatives; plus
- Business as usual (BAU, or 'walk-in'); plus
- Local marketing; plus
- Proactive sales initiatives.

It is therefore important that proactive sales initiatives support, as opposed to go against, other efforts (such as central initiatives). In addition, rewards for extra sales should be given after results of the other activities or the status quo are deducted.

Local marketing activities need to be co-ordinated with central marketing push. Sales effort should be directed towards following up local marketing initiatives. Customer needs, seasonality, product focus, company needs and contact rules need to fit together.

Cross-functional sales processes

This is a relatively straightforward item and should be done routinely. An example of a standard sales process for customer acquisition is given in Table 1.2.

Table 1.2: Cross-functional sales process example

Step	Activity	Responsibility
1	Prospect list generation	Marketing
2	List review / approval	Credit Risk
3	Direct mail	Marketing
4	Follow-up call	Call Centre
5/A	Mail reply processing	Operations
5/B	Follow-up sales meeting	Sales
6	Credit approval	Credit Risk
7	Disbursement	Operations
8	Final check, follow-up	Sales

Source: 3-i Inc.

As can be seen, the actual sales process cuts across several departments and is not restricted to Sales alone. It must therefore be planned across all the affected departments. These processes should be documented, with lead times and expected efficiency ratios. (See the following section for the importance of activity / result lead times in planning cross-departmental capacity allocations.)

Cross-functional capacity planning

This is a very important and often overlooked area, which can create bottlenecks that are hard to recognise first. The key issue is not that cross-functional capacity planning is ignored. Although this may be the case sometimes, most companies do make a conscious effort to co-ordinate cross-departmental activities – flow-through processing, hand-over points, service level agreements. The often forgotten element, in my experience, is taking into account different lead times for different activities in different departments. This is compounded by unplanned backlogs that develop when these lead time effects are not taken into account.

Case study 1: Medium-sized European bank

Here is a specific example of how things can go wrong (this is an actual recent case study):

1. Marketing plans specific central activities to promote personal loans, to be followed by credit card promotions. Marketing cross-references target segments with Credit and Sales to be as efficient as possible. Marketing also notifies Operations and Credit to prepare for increased workload. Finally, Marketing reviews plans with Sales, to plan for proper local (sales) follow-up.
2. Both Credit and Operations plan for extra volume of applications, based on past experience. Central marketing support activities start. Operations is immediately overloaded and cannot cope with the volume. This creates a bottleneck. Operations brings in extra staff to cope but still overloads Credit with applications to be reviewed, as service levels slip and exception processing is needed at higher than anticipated levels (instead of being able to rely on the highly automated credit scoring system for most of the reviews).
3. Sales starts to do local follow-up and runs into customer complaints as it takes much longer than promised to approve credit applications. In addition, it is unable to meet its sales targets because of slow central response which limits its ability to sell. The sales force is demotivated as it does not expect to achieve its bonuses.
4. Marketing does not understand what went wrong but needs to make up for the shortfall in customer acquisitions. It therefore increases the budget for the next activity, credit card sales, and brings timing ahead one week. This compounds the problems in operations, Credit and Sales. Things seem to be falling apart...
5. Review meetings are held to understand what has happened, but it seems that problems developed despite everybody trying to co-ordinate upfront.

What in effect happened was that proper lead time planning was not taken into account. Past activities by Marketing relied on direct mail, which took two weeks to start generating applications. Everyone planned based on those lead times. Marketing changed the media mix and started TV advertising. While Marketing told everyone about this, it did not mention that TV will generate responses instantly. Credit applications poured in – a successful event from a marketing perspective. But the applications came before Operations was ready. Once a backlog built up it created a bottleneck right through the organisation. When Operations was not able to deliver quality, because of the backlog, this created a credit response issue. This, in turn, created a sales issue. Marketing then tried to fix the shortfall by repeating the credit cards push, which further exacerbated things.

The key point to take from this case study is to include lead times for all activities, and their expected follow-up results, when planning capacity through different departments. Only that will ensure smooth flow-through processing. It is my experience that this is not done in up to 50% of cases, despite best efforts on everyone's part to plan activities jointly.

Components of 'sales'

It is important that a holistic approach be applied when looking at the area of sales. Different practitioners define 'sales as a total' differently. The following model is one that has been proven to work well and should bring simplicity and focus when discussing sales issues. This, in turn, is needed to engage in management dialogue – to agree on which areas to address, where effort and funding should be directed, to prioritise resource allocation, to apply fixes and so on.

The components of 'sales' are:

- Organisation;
- Management;
- Processes;
- Skills.

With the above in place, success will follow:

  - Organisation will ensure the right alignment and the staying power of best practices;
  - Management will make sure the bank has the organisation function efficiently – daily, weekly, monthly, yearly;
  - Processes will guide executional efforts effectively and efficiently, and with low wastage (which could occur if sales people had to improvise because of lack of standard approaches to different situations);
  - Skills are a basic enabler to executing the processes by sales staff.

A further breakdown of the above list is given below.

Organisation

- The right set-up;
- Alignment with the bank's overall structure (e.g. where does the call centre belong – Sales, Operations?);
- Key positions filled (e.g. sales director, head of branch network, head of alternate delivery, etc);
- Adequate support functions and staff (e.g. support team created for sales agents if it is put in place);
- Job descriptions for each position;
- Roles / responsibilities agreed;
- Performance management system in place;
- Human resource development and succession plans in place.

Management

- Planning, objective-setting;
- Co-ordinating with Marketing and other areas as needed;
- Load management, capacity planning;
- Coaching and people development / management;
- Activity planning and monitoring;
- Tracking results;
- Rewarding performance.

Processes

- By product, by channel, by target segment;
- Integrated across above elements and across functions;
- Documented;
- Broken down into:
  - Acquisition (customer and product);
  - Activation (if product is of transactional nature);
  - Usage build (if applicable, e.g. credit cards);
  - Balance build (e.g. credit lines);
  - Cross-sell (products and services);
  - Retention (active and reactive);
  - Loyalty management (building with profitable customers, managing customers out properly if needed – e.g. high credit risk).

Skills

- Product knowledge, features and benefits;
- Basic selling, needs analysis;
- Proactive and reactive approaches;
- Fitting product benefits to customer needs;
- Competitive comparisons, objection handling;
- Closing the sale, asking for referrals, follow-up;
- Handling referrals in and referrals out;
- Regulatory and process knowledge (privacy, application processing, etc);
- Facilitated by programmed and ad hoc training;
- Ongoing and periodic upgrades (by manager and by training department).

A simplified checklist to gauge the organisation's 'sales readiness' and identify priority areas for attention is enclosed as Appendix A at the end of this chapter. Readers are encouraged to modify it to their specific needs as required.

Integrated approach to boost sales efficiencies

Another approach to boosting sales through branches is suggested in Figure 1.1.

Figure 1.1: An integrated approach to boosting branch sales results

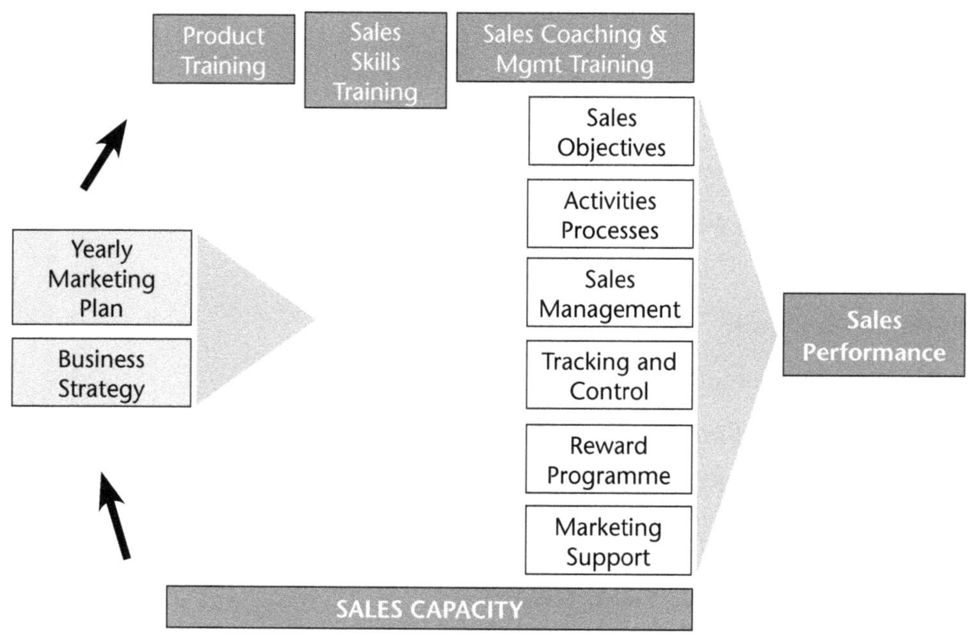

Source: 3-i Inc.

The approach works in a clockwise fashion, starting at the bottom of the figure. The whole programme is built on a solid capacity planning foundation. Business and activity alignments (with business and marketing plans) are ensured. Training is put in place to enable developing the right skill-sets. The full list of sales management and process areas is linked together, to deliver superior results at the end.

This approach is discussed later in the chapter, under 'Benchmarking – integrated branch sales boost tests'.

Yet another approach breaks down sales into its components by the areas / levels of the overall organisation that it needs to be involved with. A simplified model is as follows:

Business level

- Planning, objective-setting by channel;
- Coaching and sales management;
- Tracking and rewarding;
- Sales support and communication;
- Channel development and management.

Operational / support level

- Sales and service quality;
- Sales support;
- Processes – development, optimisation and management.

HR level

- Recruiting, performance management;
- Product training;
- Sales skills training and refreshing.

It quickly becomes obvious that the models generally address the same areas, although they may bundle them together from different perspectives. As a result, it makes little difference which model one uses, as long as it comes from a high quality source and one addresses all the elements advocated as 'components of sales' by the model.

Capacity planning

Definitions

Sales capacity can be defined as:

> *Sales capacity = (front line sales staff) x (time available to sell) + (additional capacity available)*

'Front line sales staff' means the number of those engaged in selling in the branches, call centres and agent outlets, plus outreach sales force, whether employed or agents.

'Time available to sell' is not the same as time spent on sales, but the hypothetical time that could be made available. This depends on total hours of engagement per day and on additional activities that a sales person needs to do, in addition to selling (administration, servicing, meetings, training, etc.) Note that 'sales' should be defined as all activities directly focusing on selling. This would include for example, in addition to actual selling, engaging in prospecting activities (such as list generation) and immediate pre-call preparations.

'Additional capacity available' can be generated by using third-party sales agents or similar.

For the purposes of reviewing branch sales efficiency improvements, the focus in this chapter is on capacity available through branch staff only. Adding extra staff to increase capacity is both expensive and difficult, due to space restrictions and headcount controls. Increasing working time is also usually not an option, because of legislations and contractual agreements with staff. The obvious way to increase capacity therefore is a reallocation of time to sales-related activities, away from other tasks. This requires an understanding of how time is spent (capacity measurement) and a conscious effort to change processes, activities and work assignments to free up time for selling.

Various studies, and my own investigations, show that time allocated to direct sales activities range between 15% and 45% for 'sales generalists' such as account managers in branches. The average time spent on sales is almost uniformly estimated at 20% by different sources (consultancies, market research companies, subject matter experts). It is worth noting that 'sales specialists' can spend a much higher percentage of their time on sales. However, these specialists are invariably narrowly focused, without servicing requirements, and tend to operate somewhat independently of branch constraints.

Capacity measurement

A number of items need to be kept in mind in doing this. The following sections review a simple but workable approach and provide guidelines, with special 'watch outs' noted to avoid generating misleading information. A sample tracking sheet for measuring branch capacity is included as Appendix B at the end of the chapter. The reader is encouraged to customise it for the situation at hand, for example for key activities if they differ from the headings in the Appendix.

Sample size and representativeness are the first considerations. It is recommended that five branches be used at a minimum, randomised as much as possible for:

- Perceived overall sales efficiency;
- Size of outlet;
- Type of customers in trade area (e.g. private customers, SMEs, corporate clients if applicable);
- Quality of location (high income per head versus low, etc).

For each branch, three sales persons should be used for measurement (if size permits): a good one, an average one and an under performer. Selections should be made by the branch managers, of course confidentially.

Seasonality should be taken into account. Measurements should be repeated during different time periods if strong seasonality is an issue.

Sales results for each branch (each person observed if possible) during the observation period should be cross-referenced to historical results. This is to detect any bias that may have been introduced by the measurement process and allow for correction. This can also be a useful cross-check versus seasonality effects.

Activities should be measured for two to five consecutive days. Industry experience suggests that branch productivity (defined as the average number of activities done in the branch per day, factoring out fluctuations due to staff numbers) can vary by as much as plus or minus 50% against the ongoing overall average.

A standard time sheet can be used (see Appendix B). Rather than noting the actual time spent on activities, standard time periods can be used to keep the process less cumbersome. The number of activities in each category can be tracked simply by the number of check marks under each activity during the each time period. Time periods should be small enough to provide finely tuned data but large enough to be relatively easy to handle. Experience suggests 15-minute intervals are sufficiently sized and easy to handle.

Because many different activities may be recorded during any given 15-minute period, an element of judgment may need to be applied to be able to fine-tune time allocation estimates. Weighting factors should be assigned for each activity, for translating the number of activities to time split within each period. Because the time intervals are relatively small (15 minutes), this can be done based on the combined judgment of sales staff and management. However, if needed, a separate time measurement study can be used to derive weight factors by accurately recording time spent on each activity and using the time averages to derive the needed weighting factors.

It is through the use of these weighting factors and the number of check marks (activities) that will give a good estimate of time spent on various activities.

Activities should be noted by an observer, rather than the person whose time allocation is measured. This is to ensure unbiased measuring (avoiding unconscious or deliberate skewing by the person observed when recording the data) and also to ensure that the measurement process itself interferes with the data measured as little as possible (no extra activities to be handled by the person being observed). The observer should be someone with branch experience.

Full disclosure of what is being done is mandatory for all parties: to branch staff, to customers, to management. In the case of customers, it is essential that a clear and brief explanation about the presence of the observer be given. Long explanations interfere with time measurement. No explanations would raise suspicions and may cost sales and customer goodwill, in addition to invalidating the process itself due to numerous aborted sales activities by puzzled customers.

Capacity reallocation

Rather than generating overall 'additional capacity', it is useful to discuss 'capacity reallocation'. This is because overall capacity tends to be set and generating extra capacity for proactive sales efforts thus involves reallocating existing capacities.

Not allocating extra capacity to proactive sales, yet demanding additional activities from sales staff, is far too common a mistake. Pushing responsibility back to the individual level ("work smarter, not harder") is another approach that has been proven to backfire over the years. Only by reallocating existing time, and putting a framework around it to conserve it and facilitate using it, can lasting improvements be achieved.

The process should start by identifying staff that need to be engaged in additional activities. Their activities and workload need to be reviewed and reallocations made as needed. Back-up staffing can be investigated for certain activities. Some activities might be reallocated, cancelled or scaled back.

Some banks have found it useful to split front-line branch staff into three categories, based on the level of their required proactivity, and then put 'percentage time spent' parameters around their schedules. This approach also ensures that sales staff dedicated to proactive lead generation do not get disengaged from daily branch activities. This, in turn, ensures they remain grounded in reality at the branch level and avoids generating ill-will towards them from others on the branch team.

An example of a percentage time allocation model is given in Table 1.3.

Table 1.3: Sales capacity (% time) allocation between proactive and reactive sales staff

Activity		Proactive staff	Reactive staff
Prospecting	- cold	20 %	-
	- warm	10 %	-
Call preparations		10 %	-
Sales meetings	- pre-arranged	20 %	5 %
	- ad-hoc	10 %	15 %
Reactive sales activity		15 %	50 %
Admin, other		15 %	30 %
Total time		100 %	100 %

Source: 3-i Inc.

Very importantly, once extra time has been freed up for proactive sales activities, physical parameters and boundaries need to be put around it to preserve it and ensure it is directed in the right way. This means, for example:

- Allocating dedicated time, so-called 'call windows', to staff requested to engage in outbound sales calling. This should be locked in through the branch activity plan and personal plans of the given staff;
- Allocating dedicated physical space to allow for the activities to be carried out. It makes no sense to allocate dedicated time windows if the person is still sitting at his platform in the branch and physically available to prospects, customers and colleagues. Disruptions will surely follow and sales lead generation will hardly ever happen.

Training

Overview

Sales training is a key enabler to generate the skills needed to execute the processes along the guidelines laid out through the different elements of sales management within the overall organisation, to deliver results. Some important elements of training, in addition to its fit within sales overall and its key role of being an enabler of efficiencies, are:

- It should be integrated into the overall sales efficiency push – staff trained must be expected to do better after the training than before;
- These higher expectations need to be reflected in their objectives;
- One should not assume that management knows all that is delivered to front line sales staff through training. It should be mandatory for all levels of sales management to go through the same training as their staff, if for no other reason than they need to know what they should be able to expect from their sales staff;

- Training should include outside components – no company has an overall lock on world wisdom... Management must actively look for good training possibilities coming from outside the bank's traditional HR or training areas;
- Non-conventional training may be more important for senior managers than basic courses. Interaction with outside subject matter experts (consultants, other industry executives) and attending idea exchange forums (conferences, networking opportunities) should be actively encouraged.

For the purposes of this report, however, we will focus on the more basic elements of training and their integration into the overall sales structure, rather than training at the executive level.

For each training module, a number of parameters should be defined upfront:

- How will the training be delivered? Train-the-trainer to allow local experts to spread the knowledge, or centrally controlled to ensure top quality? Train-the-trainer should be the preferred method, unless the organisation is too small to allow for it. The train-the-trainer approach is motivational to local teams, allows fresh, local, examples to be brought in, and is fast, flexible and cost-efficient;
- Who is in the target group? This must be well defined but not necessarily narrowly restricted. It can be useful to mix sales staff from different levels, backgrounds, areas to facilitate extra learning;
- Logistics – such as duration, timing, location, costs;
- Expected results – that is, what will participants be able to do differently after the training? In addition, what level of improvement in performance should be expected by management, within what period of time?

The following outline should help practitioners to design effective training programmes. It should be kept in mind that "training is too important to leave it to trainers". Management needs to drive the programme overall.

The basic sales training outline has the following components:

1. Basic selling skills;
2. Proactive sales approach;
3. Sales management basics;
4. Product knowledge;
5. Management and people skills;
6. Advanced training modules (on demand).

Basic selling skills

Target group:

- All retail and SME sales staff, branch managers and agents, sales agents and district managers as needed for refreshing. All new hires in the sales area.

Duration:

- Three days.

Expected results:

- Understand sales and service standards of the bank;
- Identify with the bank's sales philosophy (e.g. "Sales is a higher form of service", to take the fear out of selling);
- Be able to use the basic four steps of a sales dialogue:
    - Welcome customer (open conversation):
        - Approach customer / prospect;
        - Friendly, efficient greeting;
    - Identify needs (learn about the person):
        - Ask the right questions to understand needs;
        - Summarise, confirm and clarify needs before offering help;
    - Offer advice / solution (respond):
        - Present appropriate product solutions;
        - Show how product features translate into customer benefits;
        - Use support materials (leaflets, etc.) effectively;
    - Close the sale (conclude):
        - Check if recommendation meets needs;
        - Ask for the business;
        - Handle admin steps (forms, information gathering, etc.);
        - Offer follow-up, additional help;
        - Ask for referrals;
        - End conversation in warm, friendly way;
- Develop efficient skills in 'reactive' selling;
- Be comfortable with:
    - Identifying both obvious and hidden needs;
    - Being able to decide how long a sales conversation should last (is it a 'cut to the chase' quick discussion or is there time to do probing for hidden needs?);
    - Asking for the business, closing the sale;
- Know when, how and to whom to refer customers, what level of follow-up is needed.

Proactive selling

Target group:

- Same as for the basic sales skills module, but prerequisite for new sales staff is six to nine months' service.

Duration:

- Two to three days.

Expected results:

- Be able to identify customers for cross-selling and decide what products should be offered, when and in what sequence;
- Can develop proactive, outbound, call scripts and execute them;
- Ability to understand the basics of generating prospects for cold calling, developing business locally;
- Know how to support central marketing actions effectively, locally;
- Be comfortable with:
  - Making warm and cold calls, following up previous contacts made by other areas of the business (direct mail, call centre calls);
  - Leading sales discussion focusing on personal needs, e.g. housing, hobbies, children, etc;
  - Explaining future needs to be expected, even when the customer cannot readily see them;
  - Handling dissatisfied customers as a chance to identify and satisfy uncovered needs.

Sales management basics

Target group:

- Sales staff who manage other sales people.

Duration:

- Three days.

Expected results:

- Able to assess sales performance and career potential;
- Coach and develop people, address performance issues;
- Able to teach sales skills and their applications;
- Plan for and manage achievement of sales objectives;
- Lead sales meetings – daily, weekly, monthly;
- Able to develop basic local business development plans.

Product knowledge

Target group:

- All new sales staff for initial training;
- All sales non-management staff for refreshers;
- All staff for upgrades.

Duration:

- Initial training – three to four days, based on complexity of product offer;
- Refreshers – one day only, every six months;
- Upgrades as required, usually half-day to one day.

Expected results:

- Good understanding of product features and benefits;
- Ability to handle the administrative side of product sales process (applications, opening accounts, approvals needed, system input, etc).

Management and people skills

Courses should be offered to sales managers to enhance their general management skills. There are many high-quality offers available from outside sources. Interpersonal communication skills, situational leadership, effective presentations and similar training courses should be considered. In most cases it is better to engage licensed trainers from third-party providers than to develop and/or 'internalise' these courses.

Advanced training modules (on demand)

Specific, or tailor-made, training modules can also be offered, but they should be justified by demand and expected improvements in results. If the bank has an internal 'knowledge centre' or similar function, these courses could also be co-ordinated by them, by engaging highly skilled bank managers from different disciplines. Modules could be on developing local marketing plans, advanced prospecting and evaluating SME companies, for example.

Sales planning and objective-setting

Sales planning within overall sales management

Whether one considers the commonly described 'sales efficiency cycle', or the equally commonly used 'sales management cycle' model, sales planning and sales objective-setting are the starting points in both. They are therefore often separated out from the more activity / daily management-oriented parts of the full sales management process.

In terms of planning for sales results, one needs to take into account the elements that drive them. Basically, results will depend on four factors – it therefore makes sense for any planning and sales management exercise to ensure that each of these four variables have maximum values. Figure 1.2 summarises the key elements of sales efficiency.

Figure 1.2: The sales efficiency cycle

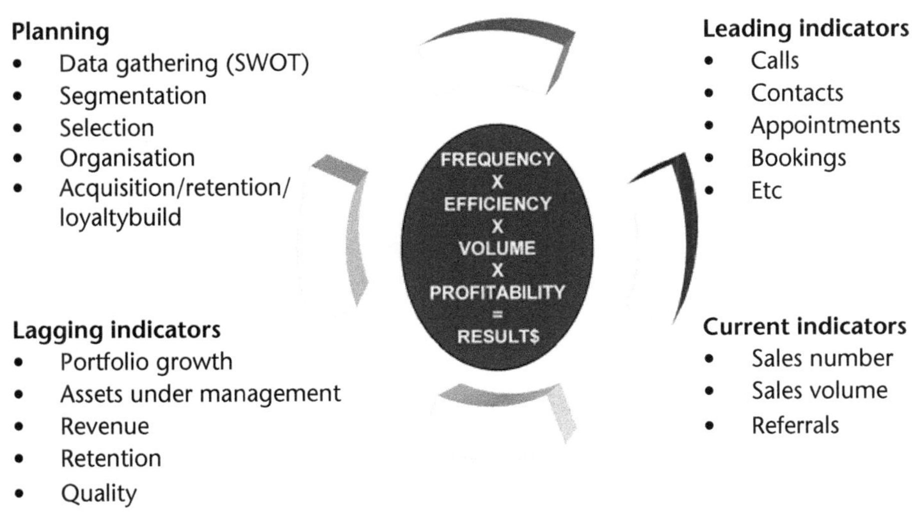

Source: 3-i Inc.

At the end, results will depend on:

- The number of sales contacts or activities (frequency) – for example, the number of incoming calls, number of prospecting calls, number of walk-in prospects, number of leads from direct mailing activities, etc;
- How efficiently one activity leads to the next level (efficiency) – what percentage of sales calls result in a contact, what percentage of contacts results in a sales meeting, what percentage of sales meetings results in an actual product sell;
- The volume, or number, of products sold during the sales meeting (volume) – the average loan size approved per sale, average deposit balance booked per sales, average number of credit cards sold and average credit line granted / utilised per card, etc;
- The mix of products sold, how profitable they are to the bank (profitability) – what are the margins, net revenues, fees, etc.

Mathematically, it is the result one gets by multiplying all these factors together that will result in profit. It also follows then that a shortfall in any one of these variables can have a significant negative impact. The sales planning exercise should ensure that each element is at its maximum efficiency (highest value). Objective-setting then fixes the expected end result in place. The sales management process (as in 'planning and managing daily activities') then takes over to ensure all the elements are linked together and executed well.

A simplified outline of the full sales management process is given in Figure 1.3. This section will deal with the first three components of it:

1. Sales planning and objective-setting;
2. Data gathering and SWOT analysis;
3. Identifying target segments and sources of business.

The latter two are integral to planning for results and should not be separated out – that is why they will also be discussed together here.

Figure 1.3: The sales management cycle

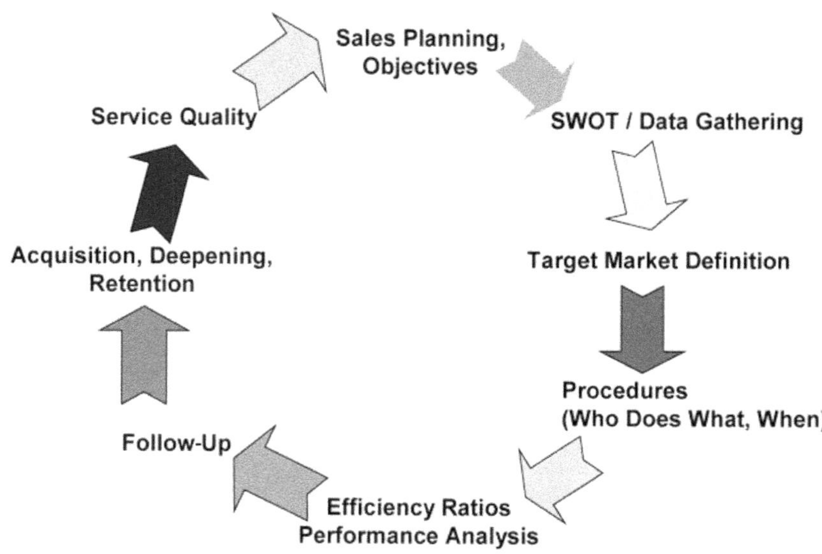

Source: 3-i Inc.

Planning the way to success

Using leading indicators and conversion ratio efficiencies will help us plan the way to success. Exponential sales growth becomes inevitable. It is thus worth reviewing them in more detail, separately, in the context of generating exponential sales growth.

Exponential sales growth happens if:

1. Objectives, plans, processes and target segments are fully aligned across the organisation;
2. A well-structured sales organisation is in place;
3. Proper sales management practices are implemented – based on the 'destination planning' approach;
4. Efficient processes exist, are followed and documented;
5. The sales force is well trained;
6. There is enough capacity in both Sales and in other departments to spend the time needed to sell.

These components are shown in Figure 1.4.

Figure 1.4: Components of exponential sales growth

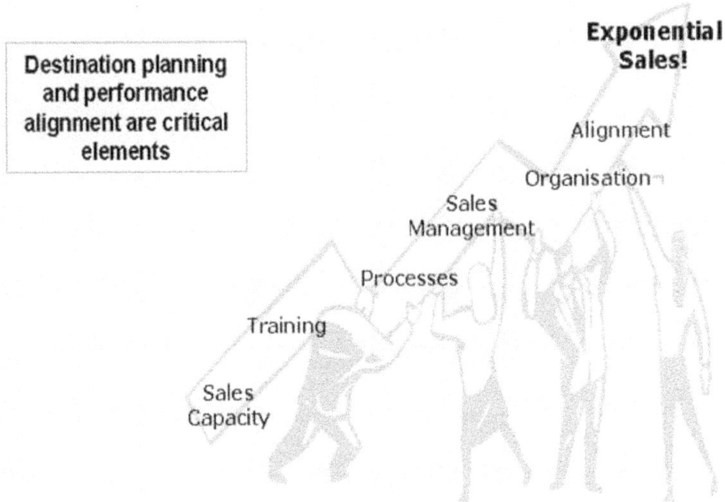

Source: 3-i Inc.

All of the above sounds very simple but countless organisations ignore one or more of them at their peril. Think about it: how many times have you seen rigorous sales training programmes that achieved nothing? The process usually works as follows.

Management decides that a better trained sales force is needed to boost volumes. The sales people are put through a thorough training exercise. Yet when they get back to their day jobs they find that they have no time for all that proactive sales effort they have been taught. On top of that, other departments are not yet up to speed in supporting increased sales activities. However, sales management already increased their targets, in anticipation of their using all those wonderful new skills they had learnt. This pretty soon demotivates even the best sales people.

Not to paint too dark a picture, but three additional sins are usually committed by management at the same time.

First, they will throw money at the problem. This usually takes the form of additional marketing spending. Without giving time to the marketing folk to come up with properly integrated plans, they are told to generate more sales leads. This will further clog up the system because capacity is still not there either in the sales area to catch the leads or in the other departments (such as operations and logistics) to deliver the goods.

Second, management will tie compensation to results. This usually happens by adding profit responsibility to the objectives of the sales staff. However, even the best sales person can not influence profitability and, hence, overall profit a great deal. How the product is priced, how it is promoted, whether a certain service is granted (for example, a personal loan by a bank) are all beyond the control of sales people. But they can, and should, sell and be incentivised to sell the right product at the right time, to the right people.

Third, management will 'stay close to the numbers' by reviewing sales results every day. Yet this really does not tell them much. They should be worrying about whether the numbers will be delivered at the end of the year, not if they were delivered the previous day. That means understanding what activities will lead to sales and making sure they happen in a well-planned, efficient way.

Examples of a 'wrong way' and a 'right way' to boost sales are shown in Figure 1.5.

Figure 1.5: Two examples of methods to boost sales

Source: 3-i Inc.

The route to planning the way to success is shown in Figure 1.6.

Figure 1.6: Planning your way to success

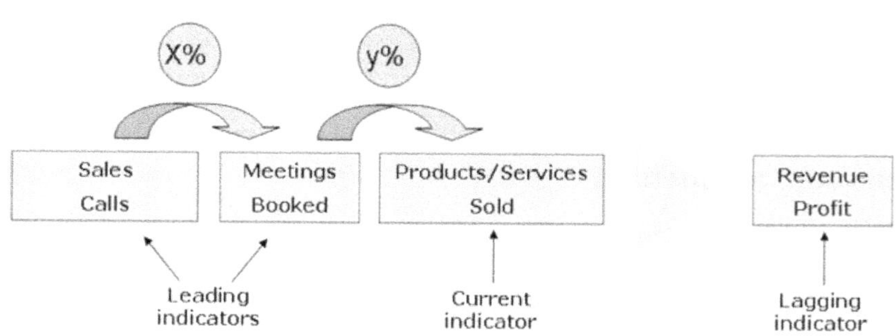

Key Steps:

1. Define destination.
2. Work back to plan steps leading to goal.
3. Track both activities and conversion efficiencies daily.
4. Intervene as needed (more time for calls, coaching for higher conversion rates etc.).
5. Enjoy the INEVITABLE success!

Source: 3-i Inc.

Leading indicators

Let's start with the concept of leading indicators. These are numerical values assigned to activities that will lead to results, such as the number of sales calls made by sales agents or number of sales meetings set up. They equally apply to other areas too. For example, leading indicators of how far I can drive my car would be the amount of fuel I have in the tank, the fuel consumption of my car, the terrain on which I am driving and my driving habits (speed, sudden acceleration, etc).

They are simple items, not complex numbers to be derived through different equations. They very much differ from current indicators and lagging indicators.

Current indicators are numerical values that tell me, for example, how my business is performing today. This could be, for example, the number of products sold at the end of the day.

Lagging indicators follow leading and current indicators and tell me about my results. The ultimate lagging indicator is my company's net profit, or any other measure / objective I have set for myself as my ultimate destination.

The problem with lagging indicators is that by the time I get them it is too late to do anything to help me do better. I may or may not have reached my year-end profit objective. But by the time I see the numbers one thing is for sure: I cannot go back in time and do better, to improve the figures.

The problem with current indicators is that they give a false sense of 'being close to the business' to management. Knowing how many widgets I sell every day lets me track my performance closely, so I can feel proud of knowing exactly where I stand on my projected sales curve. But it still does not allow me to intervene and improve the numbers.

Being able to improve my numbers, being able to 'plan my way to success' depends on tracking leading indicators and conversion efficiencies.

Conversion efficiencies

Conversion efficiencies tell me how well I transform an existing opportunity into the next one. For example, a sales call is an existing opportunity. Normally my objective for such a call is to get a face-to-face meeting with the prospect, (get him to my store, to my office, get an invitation to visit him) so that I can close the sale. That meeting will be my next opportunity. The number of meetings I can get as a percentage of the calls I make is my conversion efficiency for my sales call activity.

Similarly, how well I translate my sales meetings into actual sales is my conversion efficiency from meeting-to-sales. Example benchmarks are given in Table 1.4.

Table 1.4: Conversion efficiency benchmarks

Conversion efficiency benchmarks (%)			
	Max	Mid	Min
Call-to-contact	85	50	25
Contact-to-meeting	70	30	15
Meeting-to-sales	85	60	35

Notes:

1. 'Call-to-Contact' results depend on quality of call list – right phone numbers, etc
2. 'Contact-to-Meeting' depends on whether follow-up, warm, or cold call; strength of offer, etc
3. 'Meeting-to-Sales' depends on strength of sales pitch, product offer, sales person's ability

Source: 3-i Inc.

I can easily plan my way to success by planning my destination (desired end result) first, then working backward, using the historical date as a start, to plan:

1. How many sales I have to make;
2. How many sales meetings I need to have at an average conversion efficiency of meetings-to-sales;
3. How many calls I have to make to get to that number of meetings – again, using average conversion efficiency for call-to-meetings.

The first thing then is to check for the reality of all the activities needed to reach my destination. If it turns out I have to make 50 sales calls of 10-minutes duration per day, every day, with a 30-minute preparation time and 10-minute follow-up, it is clearly not possible, even if I were to do nothing else. (It would need more than 41 hours per day instead of the 24 available...)

If I would have to make only five calls per day (taking about four hours 10 minutes in total), then I would still need to check if this can be accommodated based on all my other activities. If not, time / resource reallocation needs to happen, or the objective must be revised.

If I am a sales manager and have helped my staff plan their daily activities, I can then follow their activities daily and can at any time tell my boss if I project to reach my targets at the end of the month.

More importantly, I can pinpoint any potential problem and take remedial steps before they threaten me reaching my destination. If one of my sales staff is not getting enough meetings set up, it is as easy as looking at his activities and conversion efficiencies to see how I can help him. If he did not make enough calls, I need to check his time allocation. Is he focusing on the right issues? Is he getting overloaded by something we did not plan for? Are his calls taking too long?

If he is not getting a high enough conversion from calls-to-meetings, I can check if the call list has the proper target prospects. I can also check if he is efficient enough on the phone. If it is the first issue, I need to talk to marketing about improving their targeting. If it is the latter, I need to coach my person in telesales techniques. The first steps in the process are shown in Figure 1.7.

Figure 1.7: Sample decision tree for intervention, tracking leading indicators and conversion efficiencies

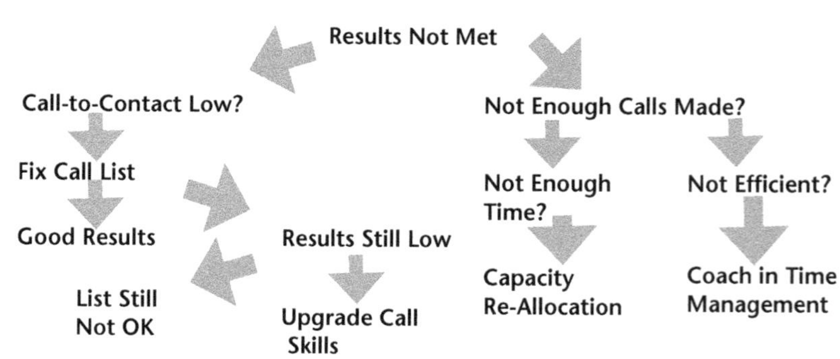

Source: 3-i Inc.

Whichever way, the key thing is that I can take action before problems arise. I am ahead of the game, thanks to following leading indicators and conversion efficiencies. I have 'planned my way to success' and control the process of getting me to my chosen 'destination'.

All this naturally leads to the question of objective-setting. While this item, and balanced scorecards, are discussed in more detail separately, it is worth mention here. My rule is never to give profit targets to front-line sales people, unless they are so senior that they in effect act like mini general managers on their portfolio of business or customers. Way too many companies hand out profit targets and call it 'empowerment', 'pushing responsibility to the lowest level' or worse...

The problems with profit targets are many-fold. Front-line sales people cannot control profit, try as they might. Therefore, having profit for a target will demotivate the best ones and will give an excuse of underperforming to the worst ones. Table 1.5 summarises the key points.

Table 1.5: Setting objectives

Profit objectives: 'Staying close to the business' or a mistake?

PROFIT OBJECTIVES

- Demotivates good performers – can't control profit
- Excuses bad performers – 'can't deliver anyway'
- Drives wrong behaviour– where is 'customer need'?
- Lagging indicator – too late to re-plan as needed
- Wastes management time – staying close to the business daily

"When all you have is a hammer everything looks like a nail"

Source: 3-i Inc.

It is much better then to stick with leading indicators, conversion efficiencies and balanced scorecards.

Alternative approaches

There are also several different approaches to traditional sales objective planning. One of these, abolishing the planning cycle altogether, will be reviewed in Case study 2 later.

Planning for objectives

- Upfront sales planning activities should include:
- Collecting relevant internal and external information;
- Analysing the information to identify key opportunities and threats;
- Identifying and prioritising target segments;
- Identifying where prospects from the target segments may come from and

how to reach them;

- Defining resources needed to take advantage of opportunities;
- Deriving goals and feeding them into the goal-setting process;
- Agreeing overall objectives and breaking them down into branch level goals;
- Communicating goals and ensuring motivation;
- Developing specific plans with milestones and expected results to deliver on the objectives;
- Putting the framework of activities in place, including tracking, scorecards, etc.

Information collecting

Internal information to be reviewed should include:

- Customer portfolios;
- Product portfolios;
- Breakdown of above by channel;
- Growth rates and efficiencies (maximum throughput rates per person, outlet, channel types, etc);
- Cross-sell rates, predictive maximum cross-sell ratios for different customer types;
- Internal developments, new capacities coming on-stream;
- Efficiency of central support in generating business, central support plans for the coming year.

External information for review should include:

- Sources of information on prospects;
- Sources of prospect contact data;
- Review of local competition, who does what well, and badly;
- Trends in the local market – economic development, new companies, real estate trends, major political changes, competitive moves, etc;
- Overall trends in:
    - The economy;
    - The competitive environment;
    - Consumer attitudes;
    - Regulatory environment.

SWOT analysis

SWOT analysis (strengths, weaknesses, opportunities and threats) looks at key internal and external factors and trends and uses them to set the best direction for the business.

Internal:

- Strengths;
- Weaknesses.

External:

- Opportunities;
- Threats.

Internal areas should include:

- Products;
- Services;
- People;
- Location;
- Marketing support;
- Processes, etc.

External areas to cover would be:

- Market trends;
- Technology;
- Legal;
- Political;
- Competitive, etc.

It is useful to have a list of ready-made questions to start the review. A reference list of questions is therefore provided in Appendix C at the end of this chapter.

Target segments

A simple definition of target segments is those groups of similar people (segments) for whom the bank is willing to pay, to make them become its customers.

How much effort and spending we should be willing to put into converting them will depend on our expected return on each new customer and our estimated chances of success to reach them and turn them into customers.

How much effort and spending we have to put into getting to them and convincing them will depend on how easy it is to reach them, offer them something superior and service them.

It then follows that defining target segments for sales and local business development activities should take into account the above factors in order to generate high levels of sales efficiencies. A standard process of defining target segments therefore could look as follows:

1. List all potential target populations in a broad geographic area around the branches. Use simple bullet points to describe and define them using key characteristics such as:
   - Where they live;
   - Where they work;
   - What their occupation is;
   - How much they earn;
   - What their family situation is;
   - How old they are;
   - If they are our customers already or not;
   - What bank are they likely to be dealing with, etc.
2. For each potential target described, estimate the potential value to the bank:
   - Size of the segment (how many households or individuals);
   - Their estimated product holdings (mortgages, loans, term deposits, pension savings, current accounts, etc);
   - The total revenue available from those total holdings;
   - What our 'fair share' of the segments should be, based on our percentage of total distribution (us and the competition together) in the area;
   - What our 'target share' could be based on the swot analysis findings;
   - What our current estimated share is;
   - What the upside potential is;
   - What it represents in terms of potential extra revenue.
3. Also list, for the same segments, how difficult / costly it may be to reach them:
   - Do we have the channel strength and variety to service them?
   - What are the best ways to reach them?
     - i. Advertising;
     - ii. Direct mail;
     - iii. Direct sales contact;.
     - iv. Offer through employer;
     - v. Other;
   - How can we get their contact details to reach them?

- What are their key needs and how well can we satisfy those with our product / service mix?
- What is the likelihood that they will come to us?
- Where do they currently bank?
- How do we compare to their current provider?

4. Give each segment a relative 'attractiveness' rating based on the above.
5. Identify what products, services, channel development, key acquisition activities we need to have to be successful in gaining them for the bank. Give a relative 'difficulty' rating to each segment based on this.
6. Compare 'attractiveness' with 'difficulty', add your own judgment and prioritise the segments in terms of where to focus first.
7. Check back against management requirements to see if we can reasonably expect to deliver the numbers if we focus as concluded.

Going through the above process will get one very close as well to delivering on the subsequent four steps in the planning process:

- Identifying where prospects may come from and how to reach them;
- Defining resources needed to deliver results;
- Deriving goals and feeding them into the goal-setting process;
- Agreeing overall objectives.

A few additional steps that still need to be taken would be to:

- Estimate a breakdown of priority target segments by competitor, define key weaknesses of the top sources (competitors) for the segment, brainstorm on how to take advantage of those weaknesses and what actions, communication one needs to initiate;
- Estimate, based on findings from the previous points 3 and 5, what extra funding or resources may need to be planned for if we wish to achieve our intended results;
- Ensure that estimated results are quantified, according to the templates / requirements used by the bank in its planning process;
- Split the estimated results (and resource requirements if applicable) among all the branches that might be responsible for delivering the sum total.

Agreeing objectives

Sales planning tends to be both a bottom-up and top-down exercise. The process described so far has addressed bottom-up planning. This is because, in my experience, it is the bottom-up part that gets ignored most, in favour of goals 'handed down' from board level. Therefore, more attention needs to be brought to it. Bottom-up planning, when done correctly, is grounded in reality. Therefore, it should never be ignored. It should be done as a reality check, if for no other reason.

The normal sequence of bottom-up / top-down planning is as follows:

- Management objectives are received and split by successive layers of sales management into channel, district and outlet level objectives;
- Planned support (extra or ongoing, e.g. additional headcount and yearly central marketing plan) are also communicated, with an indication of what they mean at each level – channel, district, outlet;
- Feedback is gathered from district level, based on the analysis described previously, carried out together with branch managers, and also on personal branch manager feedback based on judgment and experience;
- Summary feedback is discussed with management, goals and resource allocations may or may not be adjusted;
- Final objectives are communicated to everyone.

Communicating goals

Before communicating goals, a final quality check is advised on how the goals are defined. They should be:

- Clear and quantified;
- With sufficient agreement received from all key parties;
- Aligned with overall business objectives in an easy to understand way;
- Linked with logical arguments, background and historical information on:
  - Why they make sense; and
  - How they could be achieved;
- Broken down to branch level;
- Time-limited;
- Stretchable but achievable;
- Limited in number;
- Ranked in order of importance;
- With evaluation criteria clearly spelled out.

Objectives should be communicated as soon as possible. Overall district-level objectives should be communicated at a general sales meeting, which could be purposely called for this reason. Branch-level objectives should be communicated individually to branch managers. The format of the communication is important and needs preparation. Previous discussions, analysis done and feedback received should be referred to. An example of two ways of saying the same thing is:

1. *"Your objective on credit cards for next year is an increase of 15%. A bit of a stretch, but I am sure you can do it. I trust you."*
2. *"Last year you grew your credit card numbers by 12%, below the network average of 14% growth. Management wanted to see 17% growth this year. You*

and I discussed this and you made some good points about why this may be too much. However, we agreed that natural growth should be about 7%. Marketing is also putting an extra ... behind cards for next year. Based on this I believe a 15% growth rate for your branch should be achievable, with a bit of an extra effort."

The second option is obviously a better, more motivational way of communicating the same objective. However, it does require advance preparation.

Once branch level objectives have been communicated branch managers need to announce them to their staff. Objectives should be clearly broken down into key components – what part is expected to come from 'business as usual', what part should be generated mostly by central support activities, and what part is definitely up to proactive selling by branch staff.

If at all possible, sales objectives then should be broken down to individual levels, on a weekly and monthly basis. A large 'sales monitor' (board, poster) should be used to track results, obvious to everyone, displayed in a common area of the branch, such as the kitchen (not where customers could normally see it).

The branch manager should lead the development of branch-level action plans to deliver the 'local, proactive' part of the goals. This should be broken down into individual action plans and reflected in individual tracking based on scorecards, focusing on both results and efficiency ratios for leading indicators (activities) leading to them. Tracking should be done daily, with evaluations done weekly. (This will be reviewed in more detail in the following sections: 'Sales management', 'Sales processes' and 'Tracking and rewards'.)

Note that this section focuses on specific sales related objectives and their developments. However, balanced scorecards normally include related but not specific product sales-focused objectives. Some examples might be:

- People development goals (branch manager);
- Audit and control (branch manager, partially shared with others);
- Service quality and mystery shopper results (all);
- Credit quality (account managers, local credit expert if any).

Sales management

- As mentioned in the previous section, branch action plans (marketing calendars, local business development plans, etc) need to be developed to deliver on the agreed objectives.
- These need to be broken down into personal activities with personal goals.
- Central actions need to be taken into account – activities should be aligned. The BAU (business as usual) baseline should be estimated.
- Tracking must be put in place.
- Daily, weekly, monthly sales meetings (individual and group settings) have to be set up to monitor progress and ensure coaching to achieve objectives.

- Of course, proper, documented, sales processes should also exist to guide activities.

Branch calendars, branch action plans

Branches need both an action plan and activity calendars.

Action plans define what results are expected, by month, by product, by segment; and what part of those results should come from regular walk-in traffic (business as usual), from central activities and from local marketing and sales actions (that the branch is responsible for). They provide a useful overview for the manager and allow close tracking of results versus objectives. They should be further refined and turned into branch activity calendars.

The branch activity calendar should be based on the following:

- The branch's objectives for the year;
- The specific information developed during the objective-setting / sales planning process;
- Known internal factors (expected central support, their timing, extra channel support, headcount, etc);
- Known external factors (BAU baseline, market trends, competition, etc.)

Note: BAU is an important part and should not be ignored. It should also be properly planned for. Flat or 'straight-line' projections should be challenged. There should be a rationale for assumed BAU levels.

The branch activity calendar should define the actions to be taken, with enough details backing them up to be able to start execution:

- Define target segment (customer or not, if customer then what type, with which products, if not then what demographics, etc);
- Define sources (e.g. which competitor, which geographic area, where do we get contact details from);
- Define offer (which product or service, 'hook' product or standard, promotional price or not, extra features or not);
- Timing and link to central actions;
- Size of activity (how many mail pieces or calls, branch capacity to be allocated);
- Expected results – linked to the branch's objectives for the full year.

Note that there are several ways to create a branch activity calendar and various levels of depth. An overall master plan needs to be developed to give the branch manager a good overview of activities planned for the year. Plans per product (or product area), plans per segment(s) or plans per channel type can also be useful.

Plans per product or segment are especially useful if the bank has certain focus areas that it wants to address (for example, building the credit card base, or developing the premium customer segment). Creating branch plans along these focus areas ensures ongoing attention.

Plans per channel (actually, 'sub-channel') are useful if the branch has, for example, sales agents linked to it, and they may have different objectives from branch staff. An example could be when sales agents focus on building the credit card and personal loans portfolio, while the branch needs to address shortcomings in its investment portfolio.

A sample of a branch action plan (Table 1.6) and a branch activity calendar (Table 1.7) are provided to illustrate the points so far. They should present a starting point for the reader to develop his own approach. For simplicity, they are examples of activities and goals focused on a single area only – credit cards.

Table 1.6: Sample branch action plan

Branch action plan							
Branch:				XY			
Name of the product/service				**Cards**			
Period:				10			
	Months			Plan		Actual	
	April	May	June	No. Cards expected/ per action	Volumes expected/ per action	No. Cards expected/ per action	Volumes expected/ per action
Consumer customers							
central activities							
local activities							
Premium customers							
central activities							
local activities							
Professionals							
central activities							
local activities							
SME customers							
central activities							
local activities							
Total							
Total "business as usual"		200 cards					
Total "central activities"		300 cards					
Total "local activities"		500 cards					
Total Action		1000 cards					

Source: 3-i Inc.

Table 1.7: Sample branch activity calendar

Branch activity calendar										
1 Name of the product/service	**Cards**									
	Months						Plan		Actual	
	January	February	March	April	May	June	No. Cards expected/ per action	Volumes expected/ per action	No. Cards expected/ per action	Volumes expected/ per action
Central activities										
2,000 mails										
15,000 leaflets										
TV spot										
50 ads in regional paper										
....										
Local activities										
800 mails										
in-branch ads										
800 phone calls										
10 ads in local newspaper										
....										

Source: 3-i Inc.

The plans reviewed should be used to conduct both ongoing and specific, one-time evaluations of the results. These do not need to be onerous but should have sufficient detail and effort put into them to ensure lessons and improvements for the next activities. Ongoing evaluations should be part of the sales meetings (to be discussed later in this section).

Individual sales action plans

Branch plans need to be translated into individual activity plans to get to the execution phase. These individual plans (staff action plans) should define by individual contributors what they should do and when, plus what results should be expected based on the action. Expected results should first always be defined based on leading indicators – conversion efficiency ratios.

Leading indicator-based goal-setting focuses on the actions required leading to specific results. The rationale for this is that by the time revenue results (lagging indicator) are known it is too late to do anything about them. Goals have either been achieved or not. Tracking current indicators, such as volumes booked, also does not allow for timely intervention. However, one can relatively easily work back from revenue goals to volumes needed, translate that into number of accounts opened at average balances, then follow back the trail to the number of sales meetings needed to sell the products, the number of sales calls that need to be made to set up the required number of meetings and so on.

In addition, by focusing on activities within each individual's control (number of calls, calls-to-meeting conversion efficiency, etc) it more clearly holds individuals responsible for results. As a counter-example, if sales people were held responsible for revenue targets, one could argue that centrally set pricing (and, hence, spreads / margins) can sway revenue results regardless of how hard and well sales staff perform. This is counter-motivational.

Leading indicator-based goal-setting starts with the number of basic activities to be carried out, which is driven by available time (capacity). This, for example, could be the number of initial sales calls to be made. It then follows how efficiently each level of activity is translated into the next one, ultimately leading to sales. For example, what percentage of calls results in contacts, what percentage of contacts results in a sales meeting, what percentage of sales meeting results in a product sale. This should lead to volume of sales – and it is recommended that it stops there. (The rationale here is that going beyond volume, to revenue for example, will start raising the 'out of sales control' issues mentioned in the previous paragraph. This should be avoided.)

Methods and tools to be used for individual activities should also be clearly spelled out. These would include, for example:

- Whether we start with sales calls or direct mail;
- If the activity should be a follow-up to a central action or initiated locally;
- If we use direct contact, local advertising, sponsorship, organising own events, or other methods;
- How we will obtain contact information;
- Whom we will target;
- Other details as needed.

A sample individual action plan, focusing on building the credit card portfolio, is provided in Table 1.8.

Table 1.8: Sample staff action plan

Staff action plan

Name:	**Andrea**	Branch:	**XY**	Branch:	**XY**
Name of the product/service:	**Cards**	Manager:	**John**	Manager:	**John**
Period:	**From.../.../... To .../.../...**				

Description & purpose Objective:	**Method/tools to be used**

Objectives & Results	Objectives:	Results:
Calls:		
Contacts:		
Appointments:		
No of Sales:		
Volume of Sales		

Ratio's

Call/Contacts: ....% Contacts/App: ....% App/Sales: ....%

Comments on actions & learning:

Date/signature of the the staff	Date/signature of the manager

Source: 3-i Inc.

A sample tracking card, following both leading indicators / efficiencies and end results, may look like the example in Table 1.9. It can be used either for individual or group level (e.g. branch) tracking.

Table 1.9: Sample tracking card

Individual or group sales results tracking											
					Sales						
Decerr)10		Calls	Contacts	Meetings	Current Accounts	O/D	Deposits	Personal Loans	Mortgage	Credit Card	Others
	8										
	9										
	10										
	11										
	12										
Week 1	Actual										
	Objective										
	15										
	16										
	17										
	18										
	19										
Week 2	Actual										
	Objective										
	22										
	23										
	24										
Week 3	Actual										
	Objective										
	29										
	30										
	31										
Week 4	Actual										
	Objective										
Month	Actual										
	Objective										

Source: 3-i Inc.

Note that the leading indicator-based tracking, following both activities and conversion efficiencies, is also commonly called 'sales pipeline management'. It is an essential part of sales management.

Other elements

Other key elements that should be included in planning for proactive sales are:

- Referrals;
- Follow-up.

Referrals need to be included in overall plans for several reasons:

1. To allow transactionally oriented sales staff, such as tellers and cashiers, to participate in the achievement of the branch's overall sales objectives. They can do this by referring customers and prospects to account managers (customer service representatives, platform officers – the names may differ for front-line sales officers engaged primarily in selling and more involved servicing);

2. To foster co-operation among, for example, branch staff and independent sales agents linked with the branch;

3. To promote better customer service by encouraging getting the best resources involved to address client needs, instead of trying to keep the prospect / customer to have a chance of achieving an extra sale, even if the given sales person is not the best for the job.

Follow-ups are needed to close many sales sessions. In addition, they are a useful source of extra business from customers through referrals. In addition to this sales-focused follow-up, tracking may also be needed for service reasons. A basic principle of superior customer service quality is that the first bank contact person who is able to do so should 'own' the customer's problem. It then follows that this first contact should take on the responsibility of ensuring the sale or service has happened. This may not need to be done personally, but a system should be in place and the staff member owning the customer problem should be the person on top of it.

The sample contact follow-up chart in Table 1.10 shows the sales-oriented approach, to help the sales person close sales and maximise efficiencies. This should be a standard tool for every sales person with direct customer contacts. It helps them plan activities needed after initial contacts, to close a sale.

Note that contact details are included for the customer / prospect. This should also help sales staff to develop their own prospect lists, with contact details and some preliminary needs assessment already done for the potential client. This, in turn, can be invaluable for later proactive sales activities. It provides a 'warm' contact list, which should be much easier to sell to than to prospects whose details the bank purchased from a third party.

Table 1.10: Sample contact follow-up chart

Contact - Follow-up chart

Name	**Andrea**	Branch/Call centre:	**XY**
Period	**From .../.../... To .../.../...**	Manager:	**John**
To:	**Peter**	Branch/DSA:	**XY**
Sales Representative Name:		Manager:	**Peter**

Following appointments have been made

NO.	Customer Name	Address	Phone No.	New/ existing	Contact		Interest			Appointment			Source of Contact	Info on Customer	Comments	Sales		
					YES	NO	YES	Not at all	Maybe	Place	Date	Time				Product	No.	Volume
1																		
2																		
3																		
4																		
5																		
6																		
7																		
8																		
9																		
10																		
11																		
12																		
13																		

Source: 3-i Inc.

Sales meetings

Sales meetings, conducted by the branch manager, are an essential part of tracking results, giving feedback, coaching and developing people and ensuring efficient exchange of best ideas and practices. They should be motivational, focused, productive. The four key meetings that branch managers should conduct are:

- Daily huddles;
- Weekly one-on-ones;
- Weekly branch meetings;
- Monthly branch meetings.

Daily huddles

Daily huddles can be used to:

- Align the branch team behind product or service focus for the day;
- Identify immediate priorities;
- Address urgent team issues;
- Provide a motivational boost at the start of the day;
- Give a feeling of satisfaction wrapping up the day.

They should be informal, at the beginning of the day. Time permitting, they can be done twice a day, with a wrap-up added at the end. However, experience suggests that one huddle per day is enough. They should last no more than 5–10 minutes each.

Suggested approach:

- Set a certain time and place where the team will meet each morning (or after closing the branch);
- If only one meeting a day is possible it should be in the morning;
- Quickly review the previous day, its results, achievements (if only one meeting per day);
- State the focus for the day, including individual priorities and how they relate to branch goals;
- You may want to start with posing the question: "what should be our most important activities today?" to make the focusing exercise interactive;
- Provide positive feedback, reinforce desired behaviour;
- Discuss upcoming promotions, events, new products – but only the latest, most important, most immediate ones that need to be mentioned;
- Address urgent staff issues;

- Address capacity planning issues as needed;
- Mention 'news of the day' if possible – competitive, economic, consumer newsworthy items that may have a relevance on what the team should do and how;
- Ask for comments on news of the day if time permits;
- Wrap-up at the end of the day should be very brief;
- Focus on what went well, what should be done differently next day;
- Congratulate team if warranted.

Weekly one-on-ones

These are weekly individual meetings between the branch manager and key sales staff (e.g. account managers). A meeting once every two weeks should also be useful with all other staff, such as tellers and support staff. They should be scheduled in advance, for the same day / time each week. They should last no longer than 15 minutes and should always be held in private.

The meetings should be used to:

- Review the past week, including successes and challenges;
- Surface issues, problems, obstacles in a private setting;
- Review results against objectives, give feedback on current performance and recent performance trends;
- Capture best practices and reinforce desired behaviour;
- Coach, motivate, develop or discipline;
- Plan activities for the next week.

Suggested approach:

- Have a simple, standard agenda (flow) for the meetings;
- Do a short preparation for the meeting:
  - Do a quick review of the team member's results from previous week;
  - Think about any current issues and positives that may relate to the person;
- Ask for an update of the past week's sales results and activities;
- Discuss actions and expectations for the next week;
- Roll up weekly results against yearly goals and next week's objectives against the same, using your tracking tools;
- Provide effective feedback on the person's progress against longer-term goals ('effective' meaning developmental and motivational);
- Try to uncover any issues, concerns, lessons learned, ideas, success stories to share with others;
- Coach as required;

- Review what support the person may need to become more effective, and discuss.

Weekly branch meetings

These meetings should be used to:

- Review results and celebrate successes;
- Share ideas and plan for upcoming events;
- Focus on sales issues – operational concerns should only be discussed if they impact on current weekly activities.

These meetings should take about 30–45 minutes. They should be scheduled for either before the branch opens or just after it closes – the same day and time every week. First thing Monday morning is ideal, next best options would be Friday morning or Monday after branch closing. Resist the temptation to have a weekly wrap-up at the end of the day on Friday – your branch staff will appreciate your concern for their personal lives. The weekly meeting should replace the daily huddle whenever it is held.

Suggested approach:

- Have a standard, general agenda for the meetings;
- Prepare in advance:
  - Review what you will cover;
  - Make sure your team knows what they will be asked about (see 'ask each staff member for...' below);
- Review activities and results for the past week, using the branch-level tracking tools for activities, goals and results;
- Give updates on new products, product changes, new central support activities;
- Discuss actions and results planned for next week, the 'sales pipeline';
- Celebrate successes and identify areas for improvement;
- Ask each staff member for:
  - One thing they learned last week;
  - One opportunity they see for next week;
  - Any extra support they may need to realise the opportunity identified;
- Add your own comments to ideas received and summarise how the branch team should be able to deliver next week's results based on discussion so far;
- Ask for feedback on how to change the meeting, if appropriate at all.

Monthly branch meetings

These meetings should be used to:

- Roll up weekly results and look at progress against quarterly and yearly sales goals;
- Address more general issues (operational, personnel, company-wide, etc).

The meetings should replace the last weekly branch meeting every month. They should last 45–60 minutes, but not longer. Although the branch manager runs them, they should be team efforts, with involvement from all.

Suggested approach:

- The agenda should have both fixed parts and flexible slots to discuss new developments, ideas and issues;
- Prepare in advance, including engaging staff members to do their own mini presentations as required;
- Review branch results in all key areas, products and segments – how we are tracking against objectives, what we project to achieve by year-end;
- Compare with overall bank results, network averages, best branches in the network;
- Review efficiency ratios tracked, number of activities - all against plan;
- Publicly recognise the best performers – what they did exceptionally well;
- Ask the best performers for their perspective, what helped them achieve what they did, how they could help others;
- Identify key team successes for the month – discuss how team effort made them possible;
- Review key local actions, especially where results did not come in as expected – discuss why, what can be learned for next month;
- Provide overview of the coming month:
    - Key central actions;
    - Key branch goals and activities;
- Give update on bank-wide issues and developments, results and strategies;
- Address non-sales areas, such as operational or administrative issues and developments;
- Update on expected changes (if any) in the environment: competition, economy, local developments;
- Set aside time for two 'learning modules':
    - Brainstorming on local marketing ideas;
    - Skills development using role-plays.

Sales processes

'Sales process' is a comprehensive set of approaches, tools, information gathering / tracking / reporting and sales procedures that govern the bank's relationship with its prospects and customers.

The sales process should determine the behaviour of sales staff, and all others who come into contact with prospects and customers, at all stages of such contact.

Sales processes should allow for adapting sales and service actions, by channel and by individual, to specific prospect or customer profiles.

However, sales processes still reflect the bank as an organisation overall, because they depend on the bank's strategies, objectives, internal set up (channels, front-end system, operational processes) and capabilities (breadth and depth of resources).

Sales processes should be documented and reinforced in training and in daily sales management practices.

While sales processes may differ by channel, target segment and product, they should be as integrated as possible across those dimensions.

Sales processes can be split into reactive and proactive approaches. The reality of life is that, on the one hand, most sales manuals and books focus on the proactive processes only. And on the other hand, the majority of employees in contact with prospects or customers engage in reactive approaches only. It is therefore important to first differentiate between the reactive and proactive processes, and then clearly state when the greater details of the proactive process are reviewed.

In this section we will first deal briefly with the reactive process, then spend more time on the proactive approach. The reason for this is that it is the proactive process that does more for business development. In addition, it is more difficult and 'less natural' for most staff. Therefore, it needs more careful planning and reinforcing.

Cross-selling will be given special attention because it is a major part of what branch sales staff do. It is also a good 'warming up' to proactive acquisitions. Finally, it needs to be planned carefully. It is my experience that this planning stage is less understood by the financial services industry in general than, for example, planning for proactive prospecting.

Reactive sales processes

Reactive sales and service processes always start as responses to direct customer or prospect requests or enquiries. The key guidelines in managing the reactive process efficiently can be summarised in four key points:

1. Enquiries coming in at any contact point which require a time delayed response (e.g. an email enquiry through the bank's website) should always be:
    - Captured and followed up;
    - Handled through the most efficient response channel (not necessarily through the same channel they were received);

- Analysed for potential additional needs that can be addressed;
- Stored in a customer or prospect database, including contact information captured, for potential later sales opportunities.

The above should seem very commonplace. However, banks have historically developed through different silos. This means that cross-departmental co-ordination and cross-departmental processes may need to be put in place to ensure the above happen. Many times this means headcount reallocation or increase, which further complicates things.

A good example would be how to handle email enquiries coming through websites. Should they be responded to by Marketing, Sales, Operations or the Internet banking unit? Who should follow up? Who should allocate the leads? Who gets the credit for the sale? A major subsidiary of a global bank lost up to 60 qualified leads per day, for the first two months after it started internet banking operations, because it had not put in place processes to capture and follow up the large number of email enquiries it started receiving.

2. Enquiries at any contact point that require immediate response should always be turned into sales opportunities. As an example, no matter what the customer enquiry is through the call centre, an appropriate sales offer should always be linked to the response.

   If this is not possible, then the appropriate (special, new) offer should be mentioned at the end of the conversation. Never should a call centre representative simply say: "Is that all? Thank you for calling." There should always be a "by the way"; for example: "By the way madam, have you heard about our latest monthly savings plan? It is a new and very innovative offer that is only available at our bank right now. It is very easy to start up, only takes $50 per month to invest. If you are interested I can give you some information in just two minutes or send it via email."

3. If a customer wants a direct action (open an account, put money into a term deposit, take a car loan, etc) the sales person should first very quickly assess whether the customer understands what he actually wants. For example, opening a current account with a very large sum of money should prompt the question: "Sir, have you thought about maybe depositing the amount into a Money Market Mutual Fund instead? It would give you the same easy access but much better returns at this balance. I am just asking because some of our customers are not aware that this is an option and I found they appreciate it when I point it out to them."

   If in doubt, or if encountering any resistance, go ahead and execute the order immediately. Customers want quick service, not arguments.

4. Once the direct request has been addressed, the sales person should assess if the customer has time to allow exploring hidden needs that he may not be aware of, but which could be flagged to a good sales person by the request just received. For example, after a car loan application, car insurance (if offered), line of credit (if qualified for) or credit card needs (especially if an alliance card that ties somehow to automotive needs)

should be explored. If the customer has no time for this, a follow-up opportunity should be requested.

It is important that the above points be part of general sales and service training and of cross-departmental co-ordination activities.

Proactive sales processes

This process can be focused on different objectives, such as:

- Customer acquisition or upfront product sell;
- Product activation, if the product sold is of a transactional nature;
- Usage build and modification – if, for example, we want someone to use our credit card more, use it more for purchases and roll over outstanding balances more;
- Cross-sell products or services;
- Retention, proactively or reactively – note that cross-selling and providing high customer service quality would automatically address the proactive part of this point;
- Loyalty management, proactively, positively or negatively (managing proactively losing customers).

The branch sales force may come into the overall process at different points. In order of increasing difficulty, they may get involved in:

1. Closing the sale already prepared, for example by sales agents linked to the branch, who are not authorised to close;
2. Conducting the final sales session with prospects or customers already pre-sold, but who need a personal meeting for the final stage (for example, appointments booked for the branch by the call centre, as it manages central activities);
3. Following up on warm leads, either a central direct mail, or a direct mail that has already been followed up by the call centre;
4. Catching good potential prospects, who contact the branch based on central advertising or other referral programmes;
5. Following up on local marketing activities done at branch or district level;
6. Doing own prospecting and conducting the full sales process cycle, starting with 'cold contacting'.

Because point 6 is the most comprehensive and most difficult process, it should be sufficient to review the procedure for that.

This process involves five basic steps and a repeat loop. The basic assumption is that all the information gathering and planning activities have already been done at this stage. Therefore, we know what product we need to sell, what the timing would be, etc. The only steps left are the actual executional activities, with the basic pre-work and post-analysis included.

These steps are:

1. Select customers or prospects for action;
2. Prepare the first sales session (call, meeting, other);
3. Conduct session;
4. Agree / plan follow-up;
5. Analyse performance, change as needed.

Plus, based on the outcome of steps 3 and 4, repeat the process for the same prospect from step 2 – 'loop back' – and prepare for the next sales session, conduct it, agree / plan follow-up, etc.

A 'session' can be usually in this order:

1. Initial call;
2. Follow-up call or referral;
3. Personal meeting.

The minimum requirement of each session is to obtain enough information to enable future sales, some time later.

The maximum requirement (optimal case) is to close the sale during the session.

The expected 'acceptable outcome' is to take the process to the next session in a positive way. That is, a call should result either in a direct contact leading to a personal meeting, or in an agreed time for a follow-up call if the time is not right for the prospect. The follow-up call should result in a personal meeting, leading of course to a sale at the end.

Contact selection

- Should be based on the information gathering and analysis pre-work done when planning for branch-level and individual activities, supporting the attainment of the goals for the branch;
- Lists should be generated, including names, addresses, phone numbers, current banking relationship, any additional relevant information (demographic, last contact, other);
- Central support (e.g. database marketing) should be utilised as much as possible.

Session preparation

- Keep in mind expected outcome (moving to next step);
- A clear scenario should be written for every case, taking into account:
  - Greeting;
  - Introduction;
  - Purpose of call;

- Response to different objections;
- Asking for sale or appointment.

Conduct session

- Should be well prepared in advance;
- Based on scenario planning exercise (scripting, see above);
- Should be tested continuously, and changed and adapted along the way;
- The best sales individuals should try things out first;
- All results should be registered (positive, negative) with some comments to help learning.

See Appendix D at the end of this chapter for a sample scripting and scenario design exercise, to guide group activities and interactive training in planning for sales sessions. Also, please refer to 'Basic selling skills' earlier in this chapter for a recap of the four basic steps of a sales interaction or session.

Follow-up

Because the expected outcome of each session is to move the process to the next stage, follow-up steps should be agreed.

Even in the case of an immediate product sale, next steps usually need to be taken: application received, documents verified, follow-up courtesy call on service quality received, any other action.

If a product sale did not happen, the follow-up agreement should allow the sales person to take the next step and set it up in a way convenient to the prospect / customer.

Keep in mind the minimum requirement for the session as well: gather enough information to allow for a targeted product sale attempt at a later, as yet unspecified time.

A sample of contact follow-up chart has already been provided (Table 1.10) in the 'Sales management' section.

Analysis

Every action, at both branch and individual level, should be followed by a performance analysis. Results of the analysis should be fed back into the planning, training and preparation exercises to learn and improve. This needs to be an ongoing effort. No new initiatives should be planned or executed unless lessons from the previous ones have already been taken into account.

The following list of questions should be asked, and answered, to guide this process:

1. What were the conversion (efficiency) ratios and what can we learn from them? The following ratios should be tracked and looked at:
    - Call-to-contact;
    - Contact-to-appointment;
    - Appointment-to-meeting;
    - Meeting-to-sales.
2. Each of the above ratios should tell something different. For example:
    - Was the list / database of good quality?
    - Was the action well prepared?
    - Did scripting cover the most important items?
3. How can we improve the script and the scenario planning?
4. Were there any objections we were not prepared for? How can we address them the next time?
5. How did prospects react? Can we learn anything from this?
6. How did staff participate? Do they feel comfortable with the approach?
7. Do we need additional training – product knowledge, sales skills, other?
8. Do we have any issues with capacity planning?
9. How are results overall versus objectives? How much do we need to improve for next time?
10. What is the feedback from sales staff? What do we need to do differently?

Two additional, important points need to be covered at this stage: first, the importance of planning cross-selling properly; and second, the importance of understanding how the execution of the above process may differ for different segments within the retail banking target market.

Cross-selling

Branches are a full-service 'sales and service centre' for customers. Within that spectrum, however, their prime focus is usually relationship building with 'best' customers – those with both the highest profit and the highest future extra profit potential for the bank. This fits within my proposed general channel role outline:

- Acquire directly;
- Build relationships in person;
- Service remotely.

This model puts the onus of driving acquisitions on direct marketing, sales agents and the like. Servicing should be done as much as possible via remote channels, such as call centres, the internet and similar. However, for relationship building one needs the branches. Relationship building and cross-selling go hand in hand. As we understand more of our customer's needs we can offer more and more services and products to satisfy those needs.

Cross-selling improves current profits, by having the same customer have more products. It also improves retention, as studies show that those with more products and services are much less likely to leave the bank (unless of course something drastic happens, such as significant drop in service quality).

Branches therefore play a very important role in cross-selling. Cross-selling is also easier to do than cold calling. We already know the customer. We have some level of relationship with him. We can contact him more easily. As a result, branch staff also feel more comfortable cross-selling than prospecting. However, once proactive selling skills have been honed through cross-selling, they can be applied to prospecting as well. It is therefore recommended that cross-selling always be the starting point in any proactive branch sales and business development plan.

Evidence strongly supports starting with cross-selling, developing skills, then applying those skills to prospecting. Figure 1.8, from a recent integrated branch sales efficiency improvement project, illustrates this.

Figure 1.8: Results of starting with cross-selling, then using skills developed for later prospecting

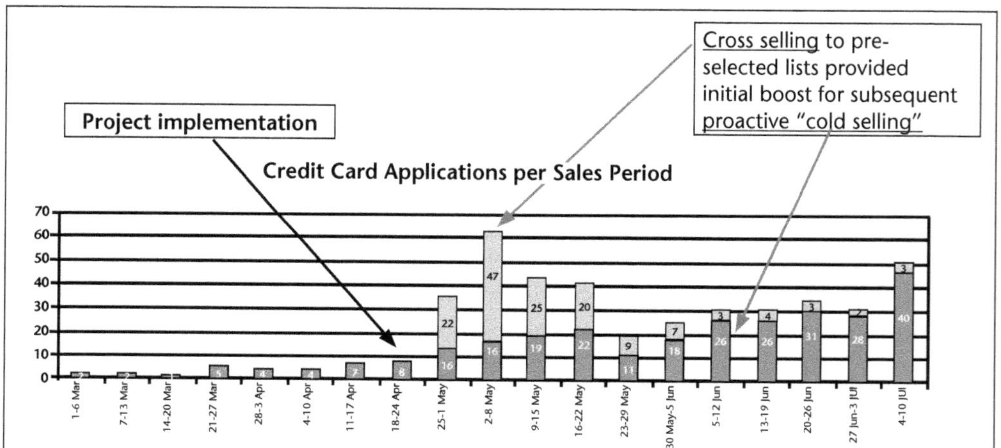

Note: Top part of bars is cross-sell results, bottom part is results of proactive prospecting

Source: 3-i Inc.

Appendix E at the end of the chapter provides an outline on planning cross-selling in an efficient way, including a hands-on guide to the 'what, whom, how, when' of this process.

Process differences by segment

Retail banking should include not only mainstream private individuals, but also the premium segment of high net worth individuals (HNWI, sometimes called the 'mass affluent' or 'future private banking segment' or similar), plus the SME market (including sole proprietors, partnerships and small businesses). The sales process targeting them should follow what has been reviewed so far. However, the execution will need to differ somewhat, in order to generate optimal sales efficiencies.

It goes beyond the scope of this book to conduct an in-depth comparison between the different approaches that need to be taken. However, a few key differences should be highlighted.

Premium segment

- Contact rules are usually stricter. It is advisable (if IT support allows it) to have a variable contact rule system for this segment. Variability should cover not only when and how they may or may not be contacted, it should also cover about what they may be contacted proactively. This may take them out of a number of standard initiatives. When in doubt, exclude them from the list.
- Only their designated account manager should contact them personally, unless the contact is a mandatory requirement and must be executed fast, requiring others to do some of the calling. This is based on the assumption that part of the premium banking package is the use of a designated account manager (if the reader's bank does not yet offer this, it should – this is the most frequently voiced need of this segment).
- Sales sessions should be held in private, not in the open area of the branch. This is yet another frequently mentioned requirement of this segment.
- Do not assume that their needs and reactions will be much different, more 'high-brow' than your average customer's, just because they qualify for premium treatment. Human needs and human nature are much the same with everyone. There is case study-level experience on this from North America. All major Canadian banks, except one, assumed in the recent past that their premium segments were not interested in low interest rates on credit cards because they could easily pay off their balances. Therefore, they should not worry about carrying charges. One bank disagreed, based on statistics which showed that premium customers carry outstanding balances to a similar extent as all others. It introduced a low-rate gold card targeted at well-to-do individuals. This became one of the biggest success stories of the decade in terms of consumer uptake.

Small businesses

Both the processes and the benchmarks are somewhat different for this segment. They are also unique because personal and business banking relationships overlap. Keeping this in mind can greatly improve their profitability to the bank.

In terms of the specific acquisition-oriented sales process:

- It pays to research their industry, not only their potential specific needs. Small business owners very much value information that can make them more successful. This can open a lot of doors;
- Be ready to deal with a gatekeeper. The chances are sales people cannot directly contact a business owner. The first step is to get past a secretary, associate or family member to get to the person you need to reach;
- Do not push for a hard close with prospects. A soft close, essentially keeping the door open for further contacts, can be a good objective for the first two or three calls. It normally takes three discussions just to build enough rapport with an SME prospect to be able to make a sales pitch;
- Always visit them on their premises to show interest, build rapport and get a better feel for their business, their credit worthiness, etc.
- The objective should be to have both the business and the personal side of their banking relationships. Experience from several markets shows significant profitability and profit increase per SME/owner when this overlap occurs.

Movement between segments

One should never look at sales processes targeted at different segments without considering customer movement between those segments. As we have seen, processes differ for premium, SME and core segments. But let us remember that many core customers will graduate into the premium (HNWI) segment.

From core to premium

Some questions we should consider:

- Are we ready to help them do so and follow them?
- Can we migrate them by offering different services to their changing needs?
- Do we know when to assign a personal adviser to them?
- Are we set up to classify them under a different segment in our database?
- Have we made sure that our own internal silos will not work against migrating them (e.g. core segment manager loses his best customers)?

If we are not ready to address all of the above, and more, we end up losing a lot of potential profit. Here is a sobering thought, from research conducted by one of the largest Canadian banks. Its premium segment manager admitted publicly: "80% of my 'A' customers (the most profitable ones) are also 'A' customers of at least one other bank." Just imagine the profit potential lost at this bank!

From micro to small, from small to medium...

The same applies to the SME segment. This is not a heterogeneous group, but includes start-ups, micro companies, small enterprises and medium-sized businesses. Unless we have well-defined migration plans and processes in place we can easily end up losing a 'micro' customer, just when it is growing into a more profitable small or mid-sized business.

Forethought is key here. One needs to define sales processes, service levels and offers for each segment along the migration path, to avoid the surprise of not being able to meet the growing needs of the client. Just as importantly, eliminating silo mentality is needed. In my experience, nothing stands in the way of good customer service in this area than the ongoing competition between retail and corporate banking segments.

As with many topics in this book, the above may strike the reader as just too obvious. However, of all the banks I surveyed, a good 70% did not have adequate migration plans and processes for their customers.

Sales process closure – 'watch outs'

When implementing a rigorous sales process in any bank, it should be mandatory to:

- Monitor customer satisfaction, ongoing – this is to ensure that customers accept and appreciate the process and the bank's drive for sales efficiency today will not jeopardise its ability to keep and grow its customer base in the future;
- Focus on the elimination of non-sales related tasks – a good sales process will highlight capacity issues and inconsistencies within the system. It will also need sales time to execute well;
- Implement a success transfer mechanism – this should be both among branches and among channels. It allows for much faster learning, fosters organisational cohesiveness and standardisation, and is very motivating;
- Make training mandatory, two-way and aspirational – good training is essential but it needs to reflect feedback from sales staff. Sales staff should also aspire to greater results, and should be given higher objectives, after training.

Tracking and rewards

What gets tracked gets attention... What gets rewarded gets done...

Tracking

The various tracking / monitoring tools need to be distilled into specific scorecards for individuals to ensure an appropriate reward system can be set up. While ongoing feedback, knowledge exchange and improvements can use the tolls discussed so far (branch plans, individual plans, activity tracking templates) a simpler, year-long set of objectives should be formalised and agreed upfront to enable efficient rewarding.

Scorecards accomplish this. Scorecards keep track of key performance objectives and allow unbiased reviews against both objectives and peers. A 'balanced scorecard' accomplishes two things:

1. Balancing the performance objectives to drive the desired short-term business orientation;
2. Mixing in non-sales related objectives (at least not short-term sales-related ones), to promote the right behaviour from a longer-term business perspective.

Balanced scorecard components

The list of headings for balanced scorecards usually covers:

- Business;
- People;
- Service;
- Control;
  - Audit;
  - Credit;
- Community;
- Financials.

'Business results' can cover:

- Leading indicators, such as early activities leading to results (number of calls per day) and efficiency measures (conversion ratios between subsequent steps, e.g. contact-to-meeting ratio and so on);
- New sales (customers or products or both);
- Retention (inverse of attrition);
- Cross-sell ratios (number of products per customer, not number of features);
- Portfolio and growth of portfolio (volume, accounts, customers);
- Referrals within the branch, to outside the branch or received by the branch;
- Revenues per customer.

Note that it is important to define what gets used when calculating cross-sell ratios. A good approach is to use the number of products per customer. A 'product' should be defined as something that can exist on its own. This is as opposed to a 'feature' which needs to be linked to a product and cannot exist alone. For example, a credit card is a product because it can exist alone. A debit card is a feature because it needs an account to be linked to – it cannot exist alone and is only an access mechanism to an already existing product.

'People management' includes:

- Self development;
- Feedback from others;
- Teamwork;

- Leadership indicators such as:
    - Employee satisfaction;
    - Turnover;
    - Percentage of promotable staff.

'Service quality' measures:

- Mystery shopping results;
- Customer satisfaction surveys;
- Complaint levels and resolution;
- Delivering on SLA (service level agreement) requirements to other departments.

'Control' variables can include:

- Process compliance – e.g. the extent to which sales processes are followed, measured by the percentage of tools described here used in the full sales management process;
- Regulatory compliance;
- Audit scores;
- Credit risk measures – only if there is local discretion in approving or turning down credit, not for centrally processed applications or applications scored locally but using centrally mandated tools.

'Community involvement' may cover various areas, from personal involvement in the local community, to being perceived as a champion for corporate ethics.

'Financial results' could include:

- Direct measures – revenue, expense, profit;
- Performance measures – ROE (return on equity), ROA (return on assets), CIR (cost income ratio), profitability.

Although very important, most sales people cannot readily and directly influence financial measures. Centrally set pricing may drive margins and fees and, hence, revenues. Head office cost allocation models may determine local costs. Bank-wide commitments or stock market sentiments may play a role. It is therefore recommended that financial results be:

- Only included for branch managers and up;
- Restricted to the functional and geographic control level of the affected managers – for example, branch operating budget over / under spending for branch managers.

Scorecard categories used, and variables within those categories, will differ at different levels. Appendix F at the end of this chapter provides a starting point on the different categories and variables that should be considered when developing a balanced sales scorecard for different positions.

Reward systems

Reward systems (sales compensation programmes) follow performance tracking as per the balanced scorecard approach described above, and ensure that performance is recognised in a way that is motivational to the recipient and profitable to the bank. Reward systems should also fit well with the occasional 'event-based activities' required for specific programmes. They should therefore have both an ongoing element (such as sales compensation system) and occasional ad hoc recognition (such as public recognition for a job exceptionally well done).

Reward categories include:

- Assigning preferred work activities;
- Intangible recognition, private or public praise;
- Tangible occasional recognition, e.g. a dinner;
- Salary increases;
- Promotions;
- Variable compensation based on results.

The last three points are strongly ongoing elements and should follow results based on scorecard tracking. The last point (results-based variable compensation) is usually the one getting the most attention and discussion time, as it forces the bank to make a longer-term discretionary financial commitment. As a result, it receives a lot of scrutiny in terms of efficiency measures, pay back, motivational value and so on. This is the area that will be discussed in some detail here.

Variable sales compensation

Variable sales compensation may account for different percentages of sales individuals, based on their role, contract, level in the organisation, organisational philosophy and market practice. The proportion of variable compensation is generally higher at higher management levels, for purpose-contracted sales staff with strong individual sales focus and in some markets (for example in North America compared with Continental Western Europe).

The actual percentage of total compensation received as the variable part will of course also depend on the performance of the individual. Higher performers will earn a higher percentage in variable compensation because they get a higher percentage of the total possible allocated compensation range, based on their results. Note that there should be no upper limit on an ongoing variable compensation programme, unless it is designed for one-time payments when pre-determined hurdle rates are met.

Table 1.11 gives some average ranges, which are examples from my experience in the various settings.

Table 1.11: Percentage of total cash compensation earned as variable component

District Manager, Europe	20%	to	40%
District Manager, North Am.	35%	to	65%
Branch Manager, Europe	5%	to	35%
Branch Manager, North Am.	10%	to	45%
Account Manager, Europe	5%	to	35%
Account Manager, North Am.	10%	to	40%
Branch Agent	75%	to	100%
Sales Agent	10%	to	85%

Source: 3-i Inc.

Variable sales compensation must fit within an overall compensation scheme and, together, they should satisfy the following criteria:

1. Make financial sense – both for the bank and for the individual. Financial modelling must be done to ensure that sales staff can in fact get more money under this scheme than under a (previous) fixed compensation plan. This is essential to motivate them. At the same time, additional spending behind variable compensation must be justified by the extra business / revenue it should generate, compared with a basic, fixed salary plan.
2. Mix individual and group elements in balance. Group level compensation helps foster team work, referrals and so on. But really good sales people are motivated by rewards at the individual level. It is usually the top 20% of sales staff that can generate 80% of the gain behind a variable compensation scheme. They need to feel motivated by a set-up that addresses their needs.
3. Drive the right behaviour. This is the essence of rewarding based on leading indicators and conversion efficiency ratios. As long as activities are directed in the right direction and are executed efficiently results will follow.
4. Cover the required non-sales areas. This is usually taken care of by basing compensation on a balanced scorecard, which takes into consideration the right non-sales areas. 'Knock-out' criteria can therefore be accommodated. For example, if a branch fails audit and does not address the issues within a predetermined time period, the branch manager would normally lose all or most of his variable compensation.
5. Have staying power. The basic system should not be changed more than once a year. Otherwise it introduces an element of uncertainty, confuses and demotivates sales staff.

6. Be flexible. While the basic system should remain unchanged, the structure should allow for layering in extra rewards for support behind special initiatives as needed.

In terms of specific design and execution, the following should be kept in mind:

1. Payments under the variable plan should be made about quarterly. The maximum attention span of good front-line sales people is usually no more than six months. They need to feel that their efforts are earning rewards in order to remain motivated. Payments should be made as soon as possible after receiving (and confirming) sales results for the period applicable.
2. Sliding-scale qualifying schedules should be put in place and communicated upfront. These scales set out what percentage of the allocated compensation will be paid based on different levels of achievement of objectives, or different levels of compliance with knock-out criteria. For example, for the knock-out criteria of audit results:
    a. If there are major audit issues and they are not fixed within two months, compensation is cancelled;
    b. If they are fixed, compensation is reduced by 50%;
    c. If there are issues but they are not (all) major and are being fixed, compensation is reduced by 20%;
    d. If there are no audit issues compensation is paid as earned, in full;
    e. If audit is impeccable and scores are in the top 5% of comparable branches, a special 5–10% 'boost' may be allocated to compensation earned.

In some cases branch level compensation may be given, instead of allocating at individual levels. This can be a useful part of the overall system, to foster team effort. But it should not be a replacement for individually allocated compensation, but it is possible that the set-up (IT support, for example) does not allow for individual-level sales tracking which is the key enabler of individual level variable compensation.

This approach is also favoured at times because it delegates local bonus allocation to branch managers. The reasons for this are:

- It frees up management time above the branch manager level;
- It is considered motivational for branch managers;
- It should promote teamwork;
- It is judged as 'being close to the action' in terms of reward allocation;
- It makes it more difficult for staff from other departments to challenge the variable part of sales compensation, while they are being fully salaried without the same upside;
- It creates an illusion of better cost control with no downside for senior management, because bonus budgets can be allocated to branch managers and

it is up to them to ensure they can motivate and reward their staff within the limits imposed.

If branch-level compensation is a must, one should still try to make it work the best possible way:

1. As a rule of thumb, about 30% of the branch allotment should be reserved for the branch manager's compensation, with 70% distributed among the rest of the staff;
2. The split among the staff should be reviewed and approved by the district manager (or whatever the layer above branch manager is called);
3. Delivery against scorecard objectives and following the agreed sliding-scale rules for allocation must still be rigorously followed to avoid favouritism.

Case study 2: Eliminating objective-setting

A large US bank tried this unorthodox approach that deserves mention here. This is a radical approach that requires careful planning. Some of its key components are:

- Ban planning and target-setting by branch. The claimed reason for this is that the budgeting process tends to take a lot of time (away from sales activities) and tends to push 'bidding down' targets by branches, so that they can over deliver and earn their bonuses later.
- Put in place a simple system, tracking how much incremental growth has been generated by each branch.
- To be fair, split branches by size (into, say, three tiers) – larger branches with large portfolios would have a harder time generating the same relative growth as smaller, newer, branches.
- Rank, each quarter, every branch within its tier versus its peers.
- Put a simple reward system in place, by tier, for all branches. Top branch managers can 'stretch' their bonuses, bottom performers are given two cycles to improve before being dismissed.
- Ensure branch managers have the authority to influence their ability to perform – this may mean hire/fire authority, discretionary pricing ability and the like.

Table 1.12 illustrates the reward system to accompany this approach.

Table 1.12: Tier-based reward system

Place within own tier	Bonus	Other
80 – 100%	2 x salary	Exemplary
50 – 80%	Yes (normal)	Encouraged
20 – 50%	No	Coaching offered
0 – 20%	No	On 6 months' notice

Source: 3-i Inc.

As mentioned before, this is a fairly radical approach, given as a thought-provoking experiment, but not advocated. This is because basic human nature (programmed in at the physiological level and thus hard to change) makes people prefer to know the outcome of basic activities, to be able to plan for them and avoid any unforeseen turn of events. As bad as constant planning may be, it is more in line with the pre-programmed human nature than abolishing it altogether.

As a result, abolishing goal-setting and activity planning should be expected to create an unacceptable anxiety level, even among top sales performers. Therefore, it should work against getting sales the efficiency improvements which depend on the motivation of each individual sales person. While the jury is still out on this experimental approach, caution is certainly to be exercised. It may well turn out to be a passing fad.

Other enablers

All the sales efficiency-oriented strategies and actions described in this chapter would not work without certain other enablers. It is therefore useful to remind the practitioner of some of the key components to be taken into account when engaging in a major sales efficiency improvement initiative.

Organisational set-up and management support

Having the right organisation in place, and having the positions filled, is a key prerequisite for most of what has been discussed so far. Fuzzy reporting lines, no clearly assigned roles and responsibilities without matching authorities will jeopardise the best laid plans.

Similarly, clearly agreed and communicated management support is essential. I agree with the Cohen Brown organisation (one of the leading sales training and sales management consultancies) in this area. Cohen Brown sometimes goes as far as refusing to engage clients unless top management agrees to support the change initiatives proposed and also agrees to actively participate, upfront in the process!

Operational processes and capacity

Executing an end-to-end prospect / customer process may start with Marketing, get approved by Financial Control, go through Credit, get executed by Sales – but at some point it will reach Operations for handling the applications, opening accounts, disbursing funds, setting things up, tracking and reporting. Without a robust operational platform, and without cross-departmental process alignments, sales efficiencies will be extremely difficult to make.

Marketing support

The central marketing plan is the cornerstone of business development activities. It should set out central actions. It should help support local marketing activities. There should be templated local marketing development activities summarised in 'Local Marketing Manuals'. Central Marketing needs to support local actions with high quality lists, database support as requested, coaching in marketing actions – the list goes on.

Channel integration

Just as sales processes cut across different channels, sales management needs to do so as well. Channel integration will be mentioned again in Chapter 4. However, it should be highlighted here that all sales and service channels need to be integrated for best sales efficiencies, in any and each of them (including branches). Channels such as sales agents, branch agents, call centres, internet, mobile phone banking, third-party sales forces, brokers and even direct mail and alliance partners should be covered. They all have different high- and low-efficiency areas. These should be listed, reviewed and overall task allocation and process design conducted to account for them.

IT support

Information technology system support is essential to enable the right sales management approach, for example by tracking individual sales and referrals, allocating commissions, delivering customer information and so on. However, in my experience, it routinely gets blamed for being a bottleneck and is used as a scapegoat. The rule of thumb should be:

> *"It does not matter what level of IT support we get. We can always do better. We can always find solutions within the given framework to improve. When IT catches up it will be nice. But we will not wait for them before we start doing things in what we believe to be a better way."*

Case studies 3 and 4: Benchmarking – integrated branch sales boost tests

I have recently been involved in driving sales efficiency improvements at a multi-national European bank in different markets. Lessons learned from these activities support the power of the integrated approach described so far and provide useful benchmarks on efficiency gains that can be expected.

Two tests were run in two different countries. In the first, a number of basic assumptions were made – essentially agreeing with local management 'wisdom' about what is already in place, the level of preparedness, executional quality to be expected, etc.

In the second, based on some painful experience from the first, all assumptions were cast aside. The full programme was built up following the principles of the integrated approach to sales efficiency improvements as advocated in this book.

Case study 3: Test 1

Set-up

The basic set-up was as follows:

- Built on sales training already done;
- Planned to use excess branch capacity;
- Assumed that 'sales basics' were in place as claimed.

Key elements of the proactive sales approach included:

- Local follow-up on central marketing events;
- Personal sales calls to prospects mailed centrally;
- Corporate employee acquisition activities;
- Proactive offers to walk-in prospects;
- Proactive, personal cross-selling to selected branch customers.

As mentioned, the test team accepted local management's perspective that:

- All staff to be involved were already adequately trained;
- There was enough extra capacity in the system to support additional activities, if only focus was provided;
- Central processes were already operating at a sufficiently high quality, so there should be no issues about quality of central support;
- Management's judgment on what would constitute 'realistic goals' for the test should be respected;
- Local objectives had already been co-ordinated with central goals and activities.

Results

Results indicated that, while the test site performed better than control, this was entirely due to extra sales by sales agents (contract sales people linked with the branch) and not by additional sales generated by branch staff. Analysis of the results also found that:

- Local management completely misjudged a number of items, including:
  - Achievable results based on original yearly plans;
  - Level of matching central and local objectives;
  - Additional sales capacity available at branch level;
  - Level of training and preparedness by branch staff;
- Sales agents 'saved the day' by taking advantage of the extra support to earn extra commission for themselves;
- Channel integration was lacking – call centre, sales agents and central marketing should all have been linked in more strongly;
- Quality of central support was below what everyone expected. Lists given to the test branch had an over 20% error rate, severely reducing call-to-contact efficiencies (to 3%, from the 10–15% benchmark set);
- Processes, especially tracking / monitoring, were non-existent, despite initial reassurances that they would be in place, on time;
- Despite all setbacks, branch staff did all they could to prove they can deliver – not because of fear of failure, but because of personal pride.

This led to the second sales test, in another market, where all elements of an integrated sales efficiency boost approach were carefully planned, agreed locally at the branch and district levels and implemented with great discipline. Local management agreed upfront to give a free hand to the implementation team to test the true upside of 'overall best practices'. To make it a 'stress test', high traffic, highly transactional locations were selected, without sales agent support – so that results needed to come from branch staff alone, struggling with a complete lack of additional capacity for proactive sales.

Case study 4: Test 2

Set-up

All the elements of rigorous sales planning were put in place:

- Upfront planning of objectives and activities, co-ordinating between central plans and local approach;
- Capacity planning and reallocation to free up about 50% of the time of about 35% of front-line sales staff for proactive selling;
- Space reallocation within the branches to allow focus for the designated sales staff, during designated times, to engage in focused proactive selling;
- Sales objectives planning, followed by branch- and individual-level activity plans and expectations, tracked by leading indicators and agreed results;

- Daily huddles, weekly and monthly sales meetings to keep the momentum, coach and improve;
- Scripting exercises and additional training (products, sales skills) as needed;
- Branch and district managers to attend the same training sessions, with objectives revised upwards compared with previous goals to reflect expected results of improved skills;
- High-quality central database marketing support;
- First priority on cross-selling to get sales staff comfortable with proactive selling, leading later to cold calling;
- First activities were fully branch driven because call centre support was inadequate. Call centre capabilities were quickly improved and their support was layered in half way through the test – with excellent additional results;
- Tracking and monitoring followed the balanced scorecard format;
- Rewards were kept at the one-time level, given the test nature of the set-up (no true variable compensation system was implemented at the test phase as it was part of the expansion);
- However, tracking and rewarding was done at the individual level, despite IT support issues at the beginning (manual tracking was put in place on an interim basis).

Results

Table 1.13 outlines the results from the first and second phases of the second test, versus benchmark and historical results.

Table 1.13: Test 2 results from phase 1 and phase 2

Phase 1	Actual (%)	Objective (%)	Past results (%)
Call-to-contact	65	50	25
Contact-to-meeting	70	30	15
Meeting-to-sales	65	35	n.a. (never tracked)
Phase 2			
Call-to-contact	85	85	65*
Contact-to-meeting	35	30	70*
Meeting-to-sales	80	35	65*

Note: * Somewhat misguiding numbers because they refer to results achieved through cross-selling, not through cold calling. Cold calling efficiency ratios had not been tracked before. They should have been significantly lower than cross-sales based results.

Source: 3-i Inc.

Note that phase 2 focused on proactive cold calling of prospects, not cross-selling to existing customers as in phase 1. This was reflected in the objectives set for the specific activities for phase 2 (which were therefore lower than actual results achieved through cross-selling in phase 1).

Business results

Credit card applications per month in the two test locations increased eight-fold during the tests' focus on credit cards, from 180 per month to 1,500 per month. On a per front-line sales person basis, card applications grew from 1.5–2 to 15 per month. Note that focused central activities also drove applications up in other branches. However, the corresponding increase in the test location was from 1.5–2 to 5 only.

Personal loan and deposit figures showed the same effects, whenever branch activities focused on a particular product area.

Customer satisfaction results

Results showed that customers appreciated the extra attention and that scripting was done right. Average customer satisfaction scores, as tracked on a scale of 1 to 5 (5 being the best) increased from 3.4 to 4.2, while control branches stayed in the 3.3 to 3.5 range. The staying power of this improvement (similar to the skill improvements carried forward from cross-selling) was shown by the fact that the satisfaction score improved to an even higher 4.4, and stayed there, upon expansion of the test (phase 2).

This is interesting, because attention for the second phase was shifted to proactive prospecting. However, it appeared that the skills instilled in sales staff to give attention to customer needs and know how to respond to them had a lasting impact. Even when they focused on new acquisition, the skills learned in satisfying existing customers stayed and bore results.

Employee satisfaction results

The test was too small to provide good readings on employee satisfaction on a quantitative basis. However, feedback has been uniformly very favourable, as sales staff became more comfortable in their jobs thanks to the processes implemented. Strong anecdotal evidence also exists to support this feedback. News of the results got out and sales staff from the test locations 'bragged' about their success to their colleagues at other outlets. This started a deluge of requests from branch managers to sales management to allow them to adapt the practices from the test locations ahead of the planned roll-out schedule. The key drivers for this were, on the one hand, requests from their own sales staff and, on the other, a recognition that the sales processes implemented could help them achieve their objectives. That in turn could improve their chances of bonuses, salary increases and promotions.

Appendix A – Simplified sales diagnostic kit

Using this simple test tool can quickly focus attention on key sales issues, in a holistic way. The best way to use it is in a group setting. Individual managers and staff first fill out the template, to be followed by group discussion.

First, rate each statement from 1 to 5, where 5 is the 'most'. For example, 5 would mean:

- "Yes, we have it completely" (reality); or
- "Yes, this is extremely important" (importance); or
- "Yes, we definitely need support here" (help needed).

Then, focus discussion on:

- Where are we the strongest and the weakest?
- What are the most important priorities?
- What are the most urgent priorities?
- What support, and at what level, is needed to improve?
- Which of the four overall areas need senior attention?

Table 1.14: Sales diagnostic template

(All four sections to be completed and discussed together)

Organisation	**Reality**	**Importance**	**Help needed**
Our front-line sales people spend 50% or more of their time selling			
We have job descriptions for all positions			
We have the sales director and key direct report positions to him / her filled			
We have recruitment and HR development plans			
Total			

Management	**Reality**	**Importance**	**Help needed**
We have a variable compensation system linked to the results			
We track performance and manage workload through leading indicators			
Our sales managers have business development plans			
We have a local marketing programme			
Total			

Processes	Reality	Importance	Help needed
We have acquisition, cross-sell and retention processes			
They are documented and our sales staff know them			
Our marketing / sales / credit / operations processes are linked together			
We catch leads at all contact points and have a process for referring and following them up			
Total			

Skills	Reality	Importance	Help needed
Our sales taff could tell me why our products are better than our competitors'			
Our staff would recommend the right product(s) for me			
Our sales people know how to handle objections			
Our sales staff would try to retain me if I was to take my profitable business elsewhere			
Total			

Source: 3-i Inc.

Appendix B – Sample activity tracking tool for capacity measurements

Notes:

1. Start and end times for the activity sheets should be early enough (e.g. 8:00 am or 7:00 am) and late enough (e.g. 8:00 pm or 9:00 pm) to allow accurate tracking of all staff activities, even outside branch opening hours.
2. A separate tracking sheet needs to be used for each day of measurement – dated, with location and person observed noted.
3. Headings across the top may vary, based on the types of activities that need to be taken into account. This should be agreed in advance with sales staff and management and be based on factual experience.
4. Weights (relative length of time) should be assigned to each activity for more precise results. This can be done based on judgment. My experience is that, with the 15-minute time intervals, weighted and unweighted results do not differ substantially at the end. A separate study to measure the actual time spent of specific activities is therefore hard to justify.

Table 1.15: Capacity measurement tool

	Meeting	Individual customer transactions	Individual customers queries	New products suggested to customers	Outbound sales calls / phone calls	New signed contacts / sold products	Appointments made	Customers got additional materials	Credit approval	Admin - no customers	Other back office functions	Corporate / SME related	Other
0800													
0815													
0830													
0845													
0900													
0915													
0930													
0945													
1000													
1015													
1030													
1045													
1100													
1115													
1130													
1145													
1200													
1215													
1230													
1245													
1300													
1315													
1330													
1345													
1400													
1415													
1430													
1445													
1500													

Source: 3-i Inc.

Appendix C – Sample list of SWOT analysis questions

Strengths / Weaknesses (internal factors, but compared against external benchmarks)

- What are the unique features and benefits of our products?
- To what extent do our products meet high priority customer needs?
- In what ways?
- Where are we better and worse than competitive offers?
- What do our customer satisfaction data tell us about where we are doing particularly well?
- Where do we need to improve?
- How does our customer base's composition reflect the bank's key target segments?
- To what extent have we been using our own customer base for cross-selling?
- What are the limits in using our own customer base for more cross-selling?
- How well are our customers aware of the benefits of our products / dealing with us?
- What is the skill level of our sales staff in the absolute?
- How does it compare with the competition?
- How does it meet, exceed or miss customer expectations?
- Is our pricing better or worse than our competitors'?
- What is the level of pricing flexibility our staff have – too much, not enough?
- How does this compare to the competition?
- How good or bad are our branch locations:
  - Compared to market potential?
  - Compared to our competitors?
- Do we have enough locations to serve the community adequately?
- What is our image in the community?
- Is our central marketing more or less effective than our competitors'?
- Is our local marketing more or less efficient than our competitors'?

Opportunities / Threats (external factors, but considering their impact on us)

- What is the impact of current economic trends on our business?
- What are the local demographic trends that could influence our business? How?
- Are there any changes in consumer attitudes that can help or hurt us?

- Are there any disruptive technology developments in the market?
- What do we know about our competitors' plans? How would they affect us?
- What are the existing strengths and weaknesses of the competition?
- Are there any local developments that can create a gain or loss for us?
- What are the political and regulatory trends we need to deal with?
- Are there any mergers and acquisitions happening that may create a threat (stronger, bigger competitor) or an opportunity (customer service problems during amalgamation)?
- Can any of the trends we looked at cross-reinforce each other? What would be their impact then?

Appendix D – Sample scenario design and scripting exercise – proactive cross-selling call to a customer

Points to keep in mind:

- Scripting needs to follow scenarios;
- All possible scenarios should be taken into account;
- Start with scenarios, add script, review;
- Even the simplest scenarios can be fairly involved – see the example in Figure 1.9, which still only addresses the upfront, very first steps, in a phone call.

Figure 1.9: Sample scenario planning exercise

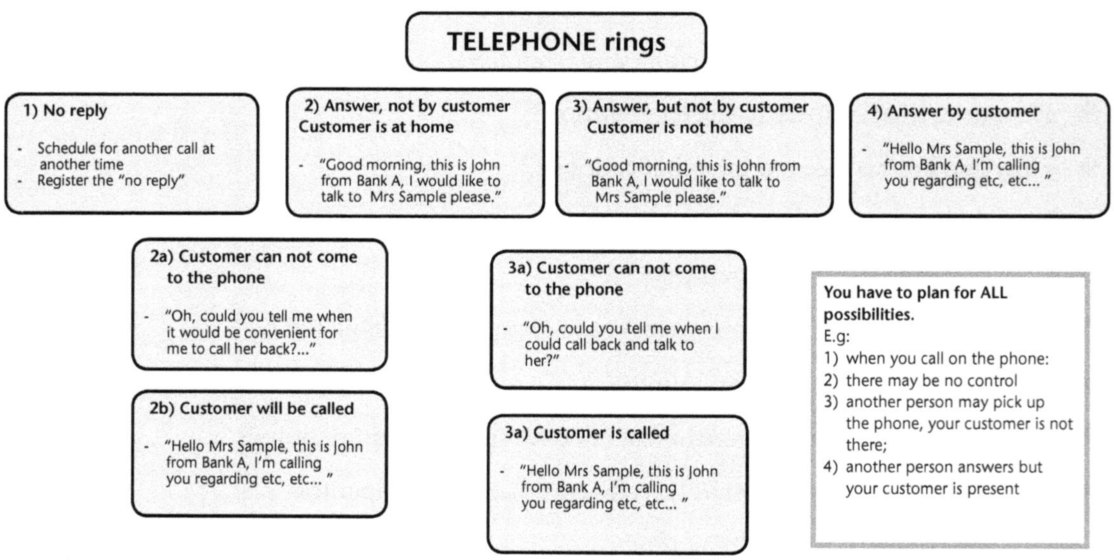

Source: 3-i Inc.

Suggested guidelines:

- Practice a pleasant voice;
- Do not rush;
- Smile while you talk;
- Try to get the customer say "yes" as early and as often as possible – do not 'attack' with questions that invite a "no";
- Always thank the customer, even if they are absolutely not interested;
- Focus on the benefits of the offer, support it with the features;
- Make it relevant to the customer, but make sure you do not make assumptions about their needs;
- Do not talk negatively about the competition;
- Imagine 'taking the hand of the customer and walking them through the conversation';
- Keep in mind the expected outcome – a personal sales meeting;
- Repeat and confirm the agreement if you reached one;
- Remember the basic sales steps when doing your script:
  - Greeting;
  - Introduction;
  - Purpose of the call;
  - Handling objections;
  - Setting an appointment;
  - Confirm and close.

Group exercise

- Objective: to design a scenario plan and scripts to go with it;
- Preparation time: 30 minutes;
- Practice (role-play): 10 minutes;
- Customer profile:
  - Mrs Anne Sample, married with two young children;
  - 47 years old, husband is a well-off small business owner (metal stamping factory);
  - Occupation: photographer, part time, but with a lot of travelling;
  - Personal income: about $60,000 per year;
  - Family income: not known;
  - Bank customer for 12 months;

- Has a current account ($20,000 average balance), started a pension plan but only invested $5000, in a deposit certificate;
- Transacts at ATMs and at the branch (infrequently), never used the call centre or internet banking.

Tasks:

Group 1: Make an appointment to start her on alternative channels;

Group 2: Make an appointment to sell a credit card;

Group 3: Make an appointment to sell investment funds.

Suggestions for sales leader:

- Be ready to answer questions on missing information – for example, has she been set up for phone banking and internet banking when her accounts were open?
- Be open to potential critique of the plan – for example why not just sell the credit card direct?
- Appreciate if teams go beyond what is required – and actually try to close a sale or use a different approach (e.g. suggesting sending an investment adviser to her home);
- Pay attention to scenario variations and how well scripts respond to them;
- Keep it thorough but light – it should be fun.

Appendix E – Cross-selling overview and templates

What to cross-sell?

- Product:
  - New – another product, account;
  - Same – increase balances, increase spending limit;
- Feature – e.g. debit card access to a current account or line of credit;
- Access – to another channel, such as internet banking, discount brokerage, etc;
- Offer from another member of your 'banking group' – e.g. an insurance or investment offer.

When to cross-sell?

- Concurrently – if there are tied needs (e.g. mortgage life insurance with a mortgage) or good product fit (e.g. credit card to utilise credit limit approved but not fully utilised by current account overdraft protection);

- As a (short-term) follow-up:
  - Plan for follow-up contact – customers sometimes just 'don't want to deal with it' all at the same time;
  - Do it within six months – expect up to 20% cross-sell success ratio, which will halve by the end of the next six months;
  - First-year attrition is always the highest, it makes sense to pre-empt it with speedy cross-selling;
- At change points – just before term product matures, when customer without life insurance turns 40, when stock markets move drastically, etc;
- Ad hoc as needed, in line with branch activity plans.

Key strategies

- Cross-sell transactional products to term product customers to generate banking activities which will tie them to the bank more;
- Cross-sell term products to transactional product customers to keep them as a customer for further cross-selling, even if they cancel their transactional product for a better competitive offer;
- When in doubt, cross-sell 'like to like': credit products to those already comfortable with credit, investments to those familiar with investing, etc.

Example of a well-planned cross-sell activity grid – targeting the branch's term loan customers

Term loan customer at the beginning of the term:

- Cross-sell transactional credit product if extra loan servicing capacity exists, e.g. credit card or personal line of credit, or overdraft protection on current account;
- Cross-sell tied-need product if warranted, e.g. credit life insurance for large loans;
- No cross-sell if obvious needs cannot be seen and/or customer has no additional debt servicing capacity.

Term loan customer around half way through the term:

- Cross-sell loan top-up (extra borrowing) if payment history is good;
- Can offer term extension if needed for top-up;
- Cross-sell transactional credit product (credit card, others) if approved by Credit Risk Management;
- Cross-sell savings or investment product if paying off loan rapidly – there may be extra cashflow that can be captured by the branch;
- Offer other loan options if paying off loan to free up debt servicing capacity for other borrowing (otherwise there is a danger that customer will leave after paying off their loan at the branch).

Term loan customer around two months before loan is paid off:

- Offer new or renewed loan if credit need may still exist;
- Cross-sell savings or investments because there may be extra cashflow, now that loan payments no longer need to be made;
- Offer line of credit or credit card if not succeeded so far.

The same plan can also be developed for other products, customers and scenarios. They can be a powerful part of the branch activity plan, especially if central database support is available or a CRM (customer relationship management) system exists that can feed the branch with prompts for cross-selling at the right times.

Product-based cross-sell grid

The grid shown in Table 1.16 is intended as a simplified template, for guidance on what normally makes sense to cross-sell, to holders of what products, in what priority sequence. It can be used in a very opportunistic way as well, when management mandate comes down to 'sell more X'. To determine priorities, find 'X' in the far left column and look across under the customer definitions. '1' will suggest the first target, '2' the second, '3' the third. Where no number appears it signifies a very difficult cross-sell. The assumption, of course, is that the 'product holder' does not yet have product X.

Table 1.16: Product-based cross-sell grid

Cross-sell the products below, to...	...customers holding:					
	C/A	S/A	T/L	L/C	CC	TD
C/A		2			1	
S/A	1		2		3	2
T/L			1	2	2	3
L/C	1		2			
CC	3		2	1		
TD	3	2				1

Product abbreviations:

C/A: Current (checking) account

S/A: Savings account types

T/L: Term loans, repaid over a period of time, with a set schedule

L/C: Line of credit or overdraft protection on current accounts

CC: Credit card (the 'true type' as understood in the Anglo Saxon world, as opposed to delayed payment debit cards, pre-paid electronic purses or similar

TD: Term deposits

Source: 3-i Inc.

Appendix F – Recommended areas to cover in balance sales scorecards

Branch managers

- Business:
  - Customer, account and volume portfolios;
  - Growth rates for the above;
  - Referrals from branch (to other areas if applicable, e.g. corporate bank, private bank, sales agents, etc).
- People:
  - Team feedback / satisfaction;
  - Turnover;
  - Promotions.
- Quality:
  - Measures as agreed (survey results, etc);
  - Co-operation with others (branches, agents, marketing, etc).
- Control:
  - Sales process tools used – compliance;
  - Audit scores.
- Community:
  - Local community involvement (one or two roles / activities agreed at start of the year, e.g. charitable involvement, sponsorships, etc).
- Financials:
  - Revenues per customer;
  - Operating budget under / over spend.

Account managers (proactive sales people)

- Business:
  - Number of calls / proactive sales contacts to be initiated;
  - Conversion efficiency ratios (meeting-to-sales, etc);
  - 3 to 4 key product sales objectives agreed upfront;
  - New customer acquisition rate.
- People:
  - Self-development (training, new skills, career progression, etc);
  - Feedback from others, teamwork.

- Quality:
  - Branch satisfaction survey results as apply to position;
  - Co-operation with others – sales agents, tellers, etc.
- Control:
  - Follows 'know your customer' rules, what can and cannot do (sales, advice).
- Community.
- Financials.

Tellers, cashiers, meeter/greeters

- Business:
  - Referrals to active sales staff in branch;
  - Percentage manual customer transactions in branch versus automated / remote;
- Speed / efficiency measures agreed upfront.
- People:
  - Self-development;
  - Feedback from others, teamwork.
- Quality:
  - Branch satisfaction survey results as apply to position;
  - Co-operation with others – account managers, etc.
- Control:
  - Percentage and frequency of cash balance outage.
- Community.
- Financials.

Chapter 2

Needs-based personal selling and the consultative approach

Summary

'Personal selling' and 'consultative approach' cover a lot of ground. It is useful to state upfront what this chapter is, and is not, about. Chapter 1 has already covered many of the general processes and steps one needs to take to master personal selling skills. These include, for example, scripting and turning reactive sales into proactive selling. Some other concepts, such as the 'seven steps to sales success' are covered in the next chapter. These areas will not be covered again in this chapter.

What will be reviewed are the specific personal steps and activities one needs to take to be able to deliver results as a good sales person, at a personal level.

We start with a brief overview of the 'Three Es principle', which has been my personal mantra defining what 'personal best' is all about in the sales area. 'Three Es refers to being efficient, effective and ethical in all sales activities.

The section on consumer needs will deal with specific, detailed items. We will review rational and emotional needs, life needs compared with financial needs, the changing time horizon of consumers in terms of understanding their own needs – and the opportunities all of these provide. In line with the importance of grounding everything in consumer needs, this section is probably the most detailed. Also, it has the most case studies, in an attempt to make the point that consumer needs should drive sales behaviour, and how best to do this.

Next comes a review of the basic concepts that cover the overall aspects of personal selling. These include the concept of 'memorable moment' on making a lasting impression, or being a 'financial physician' to always diagnose the issues before providing a prescription for them.

The section on key pointers will review some of the best personal habits of excellent sales people, with case studies to show how the concepts can be put to use.

'Advanced pointers' will review steps to be taken to be always prepared for objections, how to handle them, and how to get the most out of the information we have about competitors and the market.

The chapter closes with 'getting the most' and 'closing techniques'. These sections deal with closing sales sessions in the most beneficial way – closing the sale, setting up for follow-up sales, opening new potential through referrals, etc.

The three Es principle

The essence of personal sales excellence can be summarised as 'the three Es'. All our activities need to be:

1. Efficient;
2. Effective; and
3. Ethical.

Efficiency means how well we use our resources (time, skills, information) to achieve our goals. Items such as sales training, sales processes and time management fall under this category. These have all been dealt with in other chapters and will not be repeated here.

Effectiveness refers to how persuasive we are in our interactions with customers and prospects. In other words, can we convince them that we provide the best solutions for their needs once we very efficiently got to the point of meeting and selling face to face? This has a lot to do with personal approach and is therefore the main topic of this chapter.

Ethical selling is of paramount importance yet, in my view, not emphasised nearly enough in the different books and articles on sales. We are not talking about corporate social responsibility (CSR), which has been getting a lot of press lately. We are simply stating that being ethical in all our dealings is essential. It not only keeps us honest and within the confines of the law, it is also the best sales practice.

Customers must feel that we deal with them fairly. If we are not convinced ourselves that we are being fair and ethical in everything we do, we can never convince our customers about receiving fair treatment from us. Sales really is a higher level of service.

Sales is not about selling people what we have to, in order to meet financial goals. Sales is about helping people get what they want. It is up to sales management to set objectives for the sales staff that reflect existing and potential consumer needs and market trends. This will ensure that by helping people get what they want our staff will also achieve their objectives.

My hope is that this aspect of being ethical and putting customer needs first will clearly come through in all the points that follow in this chapter.

Consumer needs

It all starts with the needs of consumers, whether obvious or hidden. Obvious needs are the ones consumers are aware of and make us aware of too. Obvious needs may not in fact be the 'real' needs that have to be addressed. This is because consumers cannot be expected to be aware of all issues to be dealt with, especially in specialised areas such as finance. Consumers also think in terms of life needs and not financial needs. It is therefore up to the sales people to truly understand what prospects and customers need and offer the right solutions. This is what we call 'ethical selling', 'giving them what they want' and sales being a 'higher level of service'.

There are many different ways of looking at consumer needs. Table 2.1 summarises some of the best, most common ones.

Table 2.1: Consumer needs differentiation

Consumer Needs	
Several ways to define	
– Overall vs Financial	
– Life cycle based	–> product –> personal needs
– Rational vs Emotional	
– Time horizon dependent	
– Research based	–> high level –> specific

Source: 3-i Inc.

Let us now look at the different needs identification / needs definition areas and see how they can be used in personal, consultative selling.

Life needs versus financial needs, hidden needs versus obvious needs

The first thing to realise is that consumers do not necessarily think in terms of their own financial needs. Financial needs tend to come in at the end. Think of a person, for example, who needs to get to work and public transport is not available. This is a typical life need, dictated by others, such as having to earn a living. Getting to work therefore means having to buy a car. If the person does not have enough money, this will result in needing to take out a loan. Good sales people understand this and probe back in the procession of needs to uncover additional areas where we can help.

In this example, with a car loan the person may need a current account from which to pay the credit instalments. With the car the person would need insurance. If he is starting to work at a new job, maybe it would be more convenient to set him up with phone and internet banking, in case he was doing his branch banking near his previous work location. The key is not to simply provide a loan for a car (addressing the obvious need) but to probe further to uncover hidden needs which should be addressed.

Table 2.2: Consumer needs – overall vs. financial

Needs progression: from overall to financial needs	
• Base need:	"Need to get to work"
–> Facilitator:	"How to buy a car"
–> Financial:	"Need a car loan"
• Tip /advice:	
– ask questions to go back in need hierarchy –> maybe we can help with something else	
– "What else is needed with a car loan?" –> insurance, checking account, etc	

Source: 3-i Inc.

Case study 5: Consumer needs assessment

Here is my personal anecdote to illustrate how to do this right (and wrong). Many years ago we moved from Canada to Belgium. We decided to convert some of our savings Canadian into US dollars as we needed US dollars and I was going to be paid in that currency anyway. I thought I would handle this the 'smart way'. I visited five banks and asked each of them the same questions: "Do you have US dollar term deposits?" and "What are your rates?"

Two out of the five banks either did not offer the product or did not have the information (!) in their main downtown branch. One said they would get back to me. One simply gave me their rate sheet. This was a pretty disheartening exercise for someone expecting service. However, this all changed at the final bank.

The person I asked, let's call him Mario, answered: "Of course we have US dollar term deposits and I can give you all the rates. But may I ask why you are interested?" "Why do you want to know that?" I responded. "Because I would like to understand if a US dollar term deposit is indeed the best solution for you. For example, we also have US dollar money market mutual funds with good rates and liquidity. Most of my clients appreciate knowing about the full range of options. Also, most people in Canada are not interested in keeping their money in US dollars – they get paid in Canadian dollars and pay their bills in the same, so why bother?"

"OK, it is because we are moving to Belgium and need to set things up in a different currency" I said. "Ah, moving to Belgium… May I ask, is it to work there?" "Yes." "Okay, sir, I would like to suggest this: I can give you all the information about US dollar term deposits. But an international move can create a whole lot of complications which we can help you with. For example, we can set up an account for you to pay your mortgage here in Canada and have rent payments go into it. We can also arrange for you to be set up your banking in different currencies for Belgium through our Jersey Office. If you have just five minutes I can explain all of it and give you more information to read if interested. And, because you already have your mortgage with us, you are a known client so I can do all the work with minimal paperwork for you."

Need I go on? Mario did an excellent job probing for hidden needs and offering solutions, based on understanding life needs and linking financial solutions to them. We were extremely happy because one of the hardest problems, setting up banking in a new country, was taken care of for us. And Mario and his bank got our full, consolidated banking business over the following five years. And it all started with a few questions…

Life cycle-based needs

This is a fancy way of saying that people usually have different needs at different ages, at different points in their lives. The first is usually a transactional account, followed by loans for items such as a car and furniture. Buying your own place comes later and needs a mortgage for most people. As a person's earnings increase they start saving for retirement, their children's education and so on.

The beautiful thing about this is that age is relatively easy to estimate. Also, a few innocent questions (about kids, for example) can pretty much box in the prospect's place on the life cycle map. Hence, product needs can be estimated and probing offers floated with different potential solutions to needs most people would have at the same stage. Figure 2.1 summarises how key needs change over the years – something to always keep in mind!

Figure 2.1: Product needs-based life cycle map

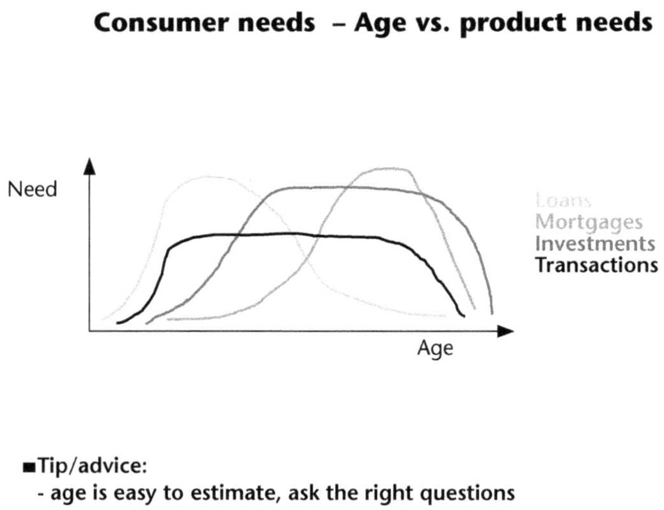

Source: 3-i Inc.

Life cycle modifications: wealth, sophistication, 'other'

Better needs analysis is possible by introducing another dimension in addition to age. For example, how wealthy someone is should dictate at what level their financial needs should be addressed, with what offers, through which channels. Table 2.3 presents just such an approach. Each life event creates new needs and opportunities. But how those need to be addressed differs greatly between the affluent and low-end segments.

Table 2.3: Consumer needs – wealth versus age-based grid

Personal needs and means based life cycle map

Age	18-25 yr	25-35 yr	35-60 yr	60+ yr	
Life	Starting out	Family formation	Career years	Retirement	
					NEEDS SUMMARY
Affluent			Elite	Good Life	Advice and tailored solutions to OPTIMISE situation (eg. Investment planning)
Mid-market		Growing	Middle	Comfortable	Simple solutions with multiple offers to IMPROVE situation (eg. Pension savings)
Low-end	Starter	Struggler	Survivor	No hope	Single offers to help MANAGE situation (eg. Car loan)
Live Event Examples	First job apt.rental car	Marriage house kids	Move schooling empty nest	Grandkids wealth transfer death in family	

Source: 3-i Inc.

However, wealth is not the only extra dimension that can be considered. Buyer sophistication and (in investment services) risk tolerance are two good examples of 'additional dimensions'. While in some cases one needs to probe and document in great detail (e.g. 'know your customer' rules for selling investments) that is not always so. Buyer sophistication is especially important to assess, so as not to offend someone by over-explaining the obvious, but also not to assume that they know more than they do.

Case study 6: Understanding consumer sophistication

Here is another case study drawn from personal experience. While it is not from the financial services sector, it illustrates the point of understanding buyer sophistication versus buyer needs and how to address them.

When setting up my own company a few years ago it became obvious that I needed a new, more powerful, personal computer set-up. Not knowing much about computers, I set out to visit a number of stores trying to understand what I may need and how much it would cost. What a disaster! Inevitably I was dealing with young, very computer-literate sales people who knew nothing about sales. They kept asking me how many bits and bytes I need, what peripherals, what connection speed – all the things I knew nothing about. Not one of them tried to understand, from my perspective, what I actually needed.

But at one store the sales person, let's call him Alan, first asked me how much I knew about computers (this was his response when I told him I "need a system because my old one is not good enough"). I honestly answered, "Close to zero. I need it as a tool." "And what kind of activities do you need a new tool for?" asked Alan. I told him about my new business. He asked whether I would want to store music on my PC (no), create videos (no), do PowerPoint presentations (yes), how many per month, how much time I would spend in front of the monitor, even if I wear glasses to read and type.

At the end he said: "Sandy, here is the system for you. Let me tell you what it allows you to do, just to make sure that we have covered everything but not over-designed it." He summarised precisely all my needs. Then he proceeded to ask me some seemingly strange questions about how big my home office would be, where I would put the PC, the monitor and the printer. It turned out he was estimating the length of cables I would need, so I would not have to come back for more...

This was already pretty impressive, but Alan also correctly assumed that I would not want to deal with setting up the system and would want the best on-site service for three years to make sure I do not lose any business due to computer breakdowns. So he had me sign up for home delivery and full installation, with additional on-site, 24-hour repair guarantee. I thought I would go around and make a decision based on the best system at the lowest price. I ended up making a decision based on an excellent sales job. I bought everything on the spot and was happy that I did not have to spend any more time being intimidated by 'techies' masquerading as sales people.

It is easy to see what Alan did right: he immediately guessed, based on my first comment that my sophistication level was low, and confirmed this in a non-threatening way. He understood my needs, both obvious (e.g. presentations) and not-so-obvious (cable lengths). He than up-sold me to installation and cross-sold on on-site service. Both of which I was very happy about. This was truly sales as a higher form of service.

Rational versus emotional needs

It is said that people buy with their hearts and justify their decisions with their heads. Whether or not this is the case for everyone, one must always keep the emotional side in mind during sales sessions. We will review the role of empathy and fair treatment later. Let us look at need definitions from a rational versus an emotional perspective here.

Ask customers what they want and they will say things like good rates or convenience. Yet we all know people who literally walk that extra mile because they always get a smile from the sales clerk at that small shop, or pay much more for a Gucci bag simply because of the prestige of the brand.

So service quality and implied benefits come to the fore. A simple way of looking at it is that we need to identify what financial solutions people need in a rational way. We then need to make sure that it is offered and delivered in a way that is emotionally acceptable to the customer.

Table 2.4: Consumer needs – from rational to emotional

Rational	**vs.**	**Emotional**
Good returns		Security
Fast transfers		Nice treatment
Convenience		Prestige

- Tips /advice:

  – Most people buy on emotions and justify their choices rationally

  – Rational / Emotional - WHAT to deliver: Rational
  - HOW to deliver: Emotional

Source: 3-i Inc.

Time horizon dependence

Good sales people can create incredible sales opportunities for themselves riding on an often neglected quirk of human nature. Our attention horizon gets longer as we grow older. Have you noticed how small babies seem to live in the moment? When mother is gone they have no concept that she will return in the future (in, say, two minutes' time) and start crying. They are fascinated by any new thing and can watch for hours. On the other hand, old people reminisce a lot and think back to times many years ago. They also think ahead, and worry about their health years in advance.

Unfortunately, in the world of personal finance, the reverse would be needed. People should start thinking early about their retirement, so that they have time to save up for it. By the time they get to the point that they realise long-term planning is needed, there is not enough time for those long-term plans. As good professionals, it is our job to be aware of this and address it. (See Figure 2.2.) We are the professionals who have the long-term horizon – it is our job. By making our customers aware of the needs they will have later on, and proactively offering ways to deal with them, we will open many sales opportunities and deliver excellent service at the same time.

Figure 2.2: Consumer Need –time horizon dependence

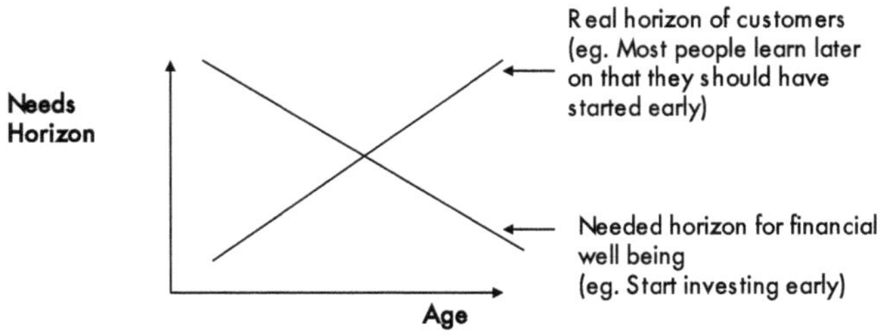

- Tips / advice
  - Bridging the difference is a great sales opportunity!
  - It is our job to know this, not our customers'

Source: 3-i Inc.

Case study 7: Time horizon planning

This is, once again, from personal experience – and this time with an extra twist. As someone who knows about time horizon issues I have been trying to deal with it in my own pension savings. Yet, someone could still teach me a new trick. As usual, I started out with a different goal to what I got at the end. My mission was to see how to get better returns from my pension savings. I talked to a number of brokers, investment advisers and banks. They all had different approaches but claimed the same basic benefits and caring attitude – nothing wrong with that.

At the same time, I have been a customer of a bank where my account manager (let's call him Aaron) was doing a good job of looking after our needs. I started with a back-up credit card and ended up with both personal and business accounts at his branch. But he knew I wanted more and correctly assumed that there was more potential from me. So he decided to go after the 'big one', my pension savings. He was very tenacious. He kept coming back, asking questions, reviewing different options with me.

He finally found the perfect pitch which, together with a good service offer, convinced me. This was Aaron's 'perfect pitch':

> *"Sandy, I know you understand investing and have been doing well on your own. I know you would like to get more out of your money saved so far. But have you considered how much time you will have to put into managing it as your portfolio grows and things get more complicated? You are entering your peak earning years and will need to focus on making money, not managing it. You need people who will professionally manage your holdings, who will look 20 years ahead and do that on a full-time basis. Yes, they will get the most out of your money – more than you could. But important thing is that you will be set up well into the future, without having to worry about things and spending time on your money when you should be making it."*

His pitch therefore brought in the element of planning a time horizon with an interesting twist, by presenting an evolving time need in my life (unrelated to financial needs) which needed to be addressed on a long-term basis. His pitch was right, the offered solution was good and my pension is now with his bank.

What does research say?

As much as research may not tell us about hidden needs, no discussion of consumer needs would be complete without a review of research-based evidence. They help with a high-level view of things while we are busily engaging in those effective personal selling steps...

Research says consumers essentially have three groups of needs that have financial sides to them:

1. Manage today;
2. Secure the future; and
3. Bring forward the future.

Manage today means managing daily life. Most things we do fall into this category. We go to school, bring up kids, eat, sleep, buy clothes, etc. Addressing the financial needs related to this includes products such as current accounts and credit cards, services such as debit cards, phone banking and the like.

Secure the future means building safeguards into our lives, so that we can predict what will happen to us or at least have some preparedness for unforeseen events. We have medical check ups, take out insurance, keep upgrading our skills so that we won't lose our job. On the financial side, this means (beyond the obvious insurance offers) having savings and investments in order to have a monetary cushion if needed.

Bring forward the future means being able to do things today that we otherwise may not be able to. We would like to get the 'benefit of the doubt' and be allowed things now that we would only be able to have without help later. We would like to have a nice car even if we don't have all the money. We would like to have our own place, even if today we can only pay the rent. This then translates into loans and mortgages, as facilitators towards later goals. We in fact are using our future earnings to have things today.

When probing for hidden needs, it is useful to keep this structure in mind to ensure we are not overlooking anything, in any of the three areas. Prevention is better than the cure, so it is worth looking far into the future, using life need probes and relying on the time horizon-dependent needs management as helping tools.

Research also says that, in terms of financial services-based needs, people also have three key demands:

1. Security of the bank;
2. Value provided – rates and fees; and
3. Service quality – convenience, efficiency, advice, friendliness.

Service quality is paramount of these for effective consultative selling. In fact, a key item in effective personal selling has to do with creating a value proposition based on it – to avoid unnecessary price discussions.

Security can be implied but one should be cautioned against using it as an overt selling point, unless working in a very unstable banking environment. Consumers tend to be sceptical when banks boast about how secure they are. This is usually followed by some bad news to the contrary.

Rates and fees can be used tactically for acquisition but they are dangerous tools and best not be relied upon.

Table 2.5: Research-based consumer needs – high level

- 3 basics needs:	Solutions
1) Manage today	Current account, bank card, etc
2) Secure the future	Savings, investments, insurance
3) Bring forward the future	Loans, mortgage

- Tips /advice:
  - Don't be afraid to talk about solutions to problems not obvious
  - Ask probing and leading questions
  - Prevention is better than cure

Source: 3-i Inc.

Table 2.6: Research-based consumer needs – specific

- Top financial services needs:
  - Security (of bank)
  - Value (rates/fees)
  - Service (efficiency, advice, friendliness)
- 'Security' is not a differentiator and should not be communicated directly (suspicious)
- 'Value' can be used to acquire customers, tactically, but not a long-term differentiator
- 'Service' is the best relationship building and retention tool
- Most people leave their bank due to lack of service and choose another based on value (service)

Source: 3-i Inc.

Case study 8: Quality of service

Another personal anecdote illustrates how service quality can save the day in the face of better price offer from elsewhere. I was working at a Canadian bank when I got a frantic call from one of our district sales managers. One of the 'Native Tribes' had won the lottery, worth in today's money about C$50m. The tribe's investment committee had visited the branches of all major banks near their reservation to find out the best rate on a three-year term deposit for the total amount.

This immediately triggered a frantic price war in the small district, where branch managers worked for years to generate even a fraction of that in deposit funds. Everyone was undercutting everyone else and offered rates that were loss-makers for the banks. The district sales manager asked me for special permission to 'offer a good rate'. This would have meant guaranteed losses for us for three years and a good chance that we would either lose the funds at the end of the term or lock ourselves into a permanently losing proposition. After all, we would have educated the tribe to expect rates beyond the reasonable, so they would probably switch if we did not carry on.

Instead, we devised a different approach. We looked at rates for annual terms from one to five years. We looked at mutual fund returns. Then we put together a response like this:

> *"We could give you good rates at the three-year term, but we would like to do more for you. So we will not propose any rates. We would like to understand how you plan to use the money and propose the best approach for your needs.*
>
> *"For example, if you think that you may need some money every year but are not sure, we would suggest splitting the funds into five equal portions and investing them in one-, two-, three-, four- and five-year terms. Then, when the Year 1 portion matures, re-invest it on five-year terms. This way you would always have some funds (20%) available to spend every year. At the same time, within five years, you would have all your money in the highest rate five-year terms, while keeping 20% liquidity each year.*
>
> *"On the other hand, if you would like to consider a longer time horizon, we would suggest taking the money you do not need in the first five years and putting it into other investments such as mutual funds or managed funds. This way you would have the guaranteed cash available as you need it, but you could get a potentially much higher return for the portion of the funds you do not need in the short run. We would of course want to understand how much risk you are willing to take with the funds and for how long you can live without them. This is for your own protection.*
>
> *"We would like to discuss all of this with you because we want to do the best for you and for your money. Giving you a good rate for three years is one thing. Being interested in your long-term well-being is another. We do not consider ourselves in the business of the former. But we would be very interested in working with you for your long-term benefit. To accomplish that, we would also give you a dedicated account manager who will always take your call.*
>
> *"We would also have our SME / corporate banking units send their best representatives from the area to review your future plans. That way, if you want to use your winnings to start a business we would already know how to help you. And you would have a banking relationship that goes beyond having a simple term deposit and works towards the future of your tribe."*

What can I say? We won the business. The other banks did not have a chance, as they focused on meeting the upfront stated demands, even at a loss, instead of thinking of ways to provide value added through superior advice and service quality. By the way, the reference to the business banking relationship also used the 'time horizon' and 'hidden needs' approach, to build a solid case.

From needs to sales – pulling it together

Targeting high net worth individuals (HNWI) and private banking prospects is an involved undertaking. It needs to incorporate the best of needs analysis, consultative selling and relationship building.

Therefore, a review of a typical high-end sales approach should give good pointers on how to mesh all those different elements together. To illustrate how this would work, the following will guide the reader through a sample five-step process. Not much commentary is needed.

HNWI investment sales – the five-step process

Overview **5-step process**
• Step 1 – Build rapport, identify wants and needs • Step 2 – Build plan to achieve needs • Step 3 – Implement plan • Step 4 – Track progress and report back • Step 5 – Identify and propose value-added services

HNWI Investment Sales – Step 1
Build rapport, identify wants and needs Gather information Exchange experiences Share knowledge Define wants and needs Define objectives Analyse current position Review current strategy Discuss obstacles

HNWI Investment Sales – Step 2
Build plan to achieve needs Define best strategies Review alternatives Design framework for portfolio to work best Share written outline of: – objectives – guidelines – procedures – tracking, reporting

HNWI Investment Sales – Step 3
Implement plan
Create investment structure Fund investments
Implement policy Implement tactics
Post-investment review Trade and settlement reports Statements

HNWI Investment Sales – Step 4
Track progress and report back
Quarterly reviews – detailed report on progress
Progress vs objectives – analysis as needed
Rebalancing as needed – keep on track or shift strategy
Annual review – overall review of both strategy and execution/results – any life events/changes

HNWI Investment Sales – Step 5
Identify and propose value-added services
Legal and accounting
Taxation
Estate planning
Advanced analytics
Family business issues
Other banking support – private banking

Hopefully all the elements have been illustrated – building emotional connection, analysing life needs, probing for hidden needs, planning a value added approach, following up and turning every opportunity into a sales lead.

Using it all – personal selling

Let us look at how all that consumer needs understanding and best-of practices from other sections of this book translate into some basic principles for personal selling. This is divided into the following key sections:

- Basic concepts – reviewing the general principles of personal selling;
- Key pointers – advice on the most effective tactics;
- Advanced pointers – being ready to handle objections and obstacles;
- Getting the most – ending the sales session with the best tangible results;
- Closing techniques.

Basic concepts

The following is a list of general principles for those practitioners engaged in personal, consultative selling. There are 10 key concepts to remember. This is a reminder list only – those wanting to learn more about them are encouraged to review any list of basic sales skills offers. Good sources of information would include Cohen Brown in the US and the Garrison Group in Europe (no, they are not paying me for this).

1) Selling

As discussed before, selling is a higher form of service. It is helping people get what they need. Let us never forget it.

2) Reality

Reality is as it is. You can argue whether gravity exists, but will still fall on your face if you trip up. Ignoring reality is a cardinal sin. Competition is getting tougher – that is its job. Others are not playing fair – it happens. Someone is always more desperate and throws money at it – that is life. The sooner we stop making excuses for our difficulties, the better we will be prepared to address them.

3) Memorable moment

Every time you meet a prospect or a client is your best / last chance to make a memorable impression. You should always try to do your best. If the customer walks away today, what impression would he carry? Would he recommend you to his friends?

4) Financial physicians

A good bank sales person is like a 'financial physician'. A physician would never prescribe a medication without completing a diagnosis first. Step one: identify the symptoms; step 2: diagnose the cause; step 3: suggest remedy / solution. This is the same in both healthcare and financial services.

5) Empathy and understanding

These are key. First, your mind needs to be open to input if you wish to understand the customer's needs. Second, you need to project that you are treating your customers with dignity and respect.

6) Respect

Respect your prospects' / customers' expertise in their professions and their life experience. But do not be shy about stating your own skills. This goes back to the concepts of time horizon dependence and being a financial physician.

7) Responsibility

In line with the above suggestion, make sure your clients understand your role and responsibility. It is best to state this in very straightforward language that suggests you are taking responsibility for their needs.

For example: "I consider it to be my responsibility to help you keep, grow and use your money in the most efficient way." Or: "I take it as my responsibility to make sure you get the funding you need for your investment and business activities, while not putting you in undue danger of being unable to repay your obligations."

8) Basic skills

We all learn to clarify and confirm. But how many times do we practice it in the heat of the moment? Let us use them for good results.

9) 'You just never know'

Going back to the 'Respect' heading – you never know who is walking in through the branch door. Treat all with the respect due to every human being.

10) Engagement

If you are not excited about your job, about your offer, about your help – why should you expect anyone else to be? If you believe in what you say, show it. Be engaging. As was once said: "You can not bore people to greatness." Similarly, you certainly cannot bore your prospects into buying your proposal!

Key pointers

Key pointers are essential sales tricks that the best develop over time. A brief summary may help you get ahead in the game by considering some good practices to accelerate your sales progress. Although we used the word 'tricks' above, it was used to describe a simple but effective approach. It should not be confused with tricking anyone into buying anything he/she does not need. That would go against the 'ethical' selling part of the "Three Es" principle and is to be avoided at all costs.

1) Review the situation

Amply covered in the 'Needs' section earlier. One must look at all needs, not only the obvious financial services-related ones. An interesting twist on this is how far one should go in offering help with other needs, not linked in any way to financial offers. This would include, in the extreme, where the best kindergarten is, restaurant recommendations, travel trips, etc.

The rule of thumb is that the higher one goes in the client segment hierarchy, the more this may be needed. Private bankers may routinely be asked for advice unrelated to their specific areas of financial expertise. On the other hand, in standard consumer banking practice some small, personal advice to build rapport should do. There is no need to go beyond this, as it may go against the 'treat with respect' principle.

2) Killer silence

Be prepared for, and try to avoid, killer silences. The easiest way around them is to avoid questions which invite a simple yes / no answer. Those questions do not unearth much extra information. For example, instead of asking "Is there anything else I can do for you?" say "I see that you have just recently moved. That creates a lot of issues. Which parts of your move-related financial obligations have you already covered? I may be able to help with the rest."

3) Story telling

Try to wrap stories around your openings and proposals. A proven way of doing this is referring to previous experience with clients. Remember the story of Mario from earlier on? He was saying: "Most of my clients appreciate knowing about the full range of options." This is a classic way of pulling prospects in. Be ready to talk about "one of my clients in a similar situation found it useful to…" or "some people I met with similar issues thought that…"

In any case, build a story. People remember stories and engage with them.

4) The power of numbers

Marketing research shows that any bank advertising with an interest rate in it is remembered by twice as many people than the same without a number. But not all numbers are the same. Obscure percentages may not cut it. You should use absolute numbers as much as possible and roll them up to a meaningful level. So, instead of saying "you can save 0.25% with our rate", say "you will save €238 per month with our rate." Or, if it is only €20 per month, state "you will save €240 each year". Or, if it is €6 per month on a seven-year loan, state "you will be €504 ahead at the end of your loan."

5) Take responsibility – again

If you do not have the answer to a question, admit it. But take responsibility for finding out and getting back to the customer, within a specified time frame. This will show him you are in charge, take an interest in his affairs and he should be dealing with you to avoid the run-around he would get at other banks.

6) 'Elevator speech'

Job applicants are routinely told by recruiters to practice 'elevator speeches'. The story goes like this: "Imagine that you are in an elevator with the CEO of the company where you are applying for a job. You have 30 seconds to tell him about yourself and convince him his company should hire you. What would you say?"

This will force you to prepare a base essential summary of why prospects should deal with your bank and yourself. Keep honing it. The key idea is to get different concepts across in a bullet pointed, telegraphic way – hard-hitting, clear, convincing, with the right balance of information and convincing benefits.

7) Never do cold calls

One of the most important key pointers. But what does it mean? Does it make any sense? Shouldn't sales people do prospecting? How do you go about acquiring new customers without 'cold calling'?

Yes, it does make sense. The objective should be to always 'warm up' a prospect before we spend valuable sales time on a personal contact. This makes sense from both the bank's and the consumer's perspective. True cold calling does not allow for needs identification upfront and hence has a high probability of getting the offer wrong. This is annoying to the prospect and demotivating (because of the inevitable rejection) to the sales person.

If we believe in putting the customer first, if we believe that 'sales is a higher level of service', we should always try to do a needs analysis first. This can be done using other channels – direct mail first, call centre follow-up next and only then a sales call. Often the self-selection of prospects acts as a needs analysis – only those who are interested would agree to a follow up contact. Our objective should always be to avoid cold calling and getting prospects' permission for the 'next contact' as part of a well-planned acquisition process.

Table 2.7: Never do cold calls!

- **High rejection rates**
  - Low efficiency
  - Demotivation
- **Low probability of getting needs right**
  - No service, no sales
  - Annoying to prospects
- **Put consumers first**
  - Test for needs
  - Warm up, "get permission"

Source: 3-i Inc.

Advanced pointers

This section deals with being prepared for objections and handling them in the most effective way. As we will see, handling objections is not an issue for the moment when an objection comes up. It is a question of preparation, of being aware of competitive offers, of being ready to move. Muhammad Ali once said the outcome of a title fight is not decided in the ring. It is decided in the gym, during the six months of preparations for the fight. By the time the actual fight happens, it is all decided. The one with the better preparation will win.

1) Negative feedback

Negatives will come at you from those you are trying to sell to. Sometimes they are well-founded issues. Sometimes they are a request for more information. Sometimes they are an attempt to wear you down on price or other conditions. In all cases, we need to keep three things in mind:

- Always expect negatives, objections – be prepared;
- Always try to understand what the real issue is – probe, clarify; and
- Always focus on the value we provide as the most efficient way of addressing issues.

Let us take a look at some common negative feedback:

"You are just saying this to... (sell me something)"

If we did our needs analysis right and followed the ethical selling principles, this is an easy objection to handle. All we need to do is to go back through the line we followed to get us to the sales proposal and see if our joint logic with the prospect still holds true. If it does, it will prove once again the value of our proposal. If it does not, then we will learn important information that had not come up before. This will allow us to refine, change and improve our selling proposal, demonstrating our flexible approach and the fact that we always keep the customer's needs at the forefront.

"Why are you not giving me the loan I asked for?"

The key here is again to explain that our credit decisions are there to protect the customer. Surely, they protect the bank too, but if one of many thousands of customers defaults on his loan, the bank will not go bankrupt. On the other hand, if the customer we are talking to is unable to pay his loan he may lose the car, the TV or the house he bought, or he may actually have to declare personal bankruptcy.

These are the dangers we are trying to avoid for him. We are experts in this area and can assess his ability to repay the loan based on our experience. It is therefore our responsibility to 'save him from himself', even if we have to decline the opportunity to give him a loan (and make money on it).

"I don't need insurance with my loan – why are you insisting on it?"

The answer to this objection goes back to the previous point. The idea is to ensure peace of mind for the customer, to make sure that if anything happens to him he (or his family if he dies) does not end up losing his possessions, on top of the other unfortunate things.

"Your rate is too high / too low / worse than the competition's"

First, if the reference to the competition is not correct, let us simply state that and offer our competitive review as proof. Let us also make sure we compare apples with apples. Many times consumers do not understand the full product offers with all the benefits and features attached and compare prices only. Reviewing what we are providing versus the competition, at what rates and fees will start refocusing the conversation where it should be: on value, not on price.

This objection can also bring up hidden information. Current accounts, for example, are not designed for savings. They provide low rates and often carry extra fees. But they also provide instant access, transfer capability, payment card options – the list goes on. If rates are the issue then a savings account should also be considered and the funds split.

2) Handling objections

An objection is a stronger form of negative feedback. The person we are talking with appears to be rejecting our proposal, not just questioning it or stating negatives. However, responding well to negative feedback (see above) is 90% of the success behind handling any objection.

The key item to remember is that objections are normal. They do not necessarily mean a rejection of the sale. Objections may be informed or uninformed. They may just be instinctive – especially if the customer does not believe the proposal. (Too good to be true – where is the catch?) Our response to them needs to make sure that:

- We understand what is being objected and why before we address the objection; and
- We also keep in mind that objections are not personal, directed at us – we should never allow ourselves to take it personally and risk turning them into a real personal issue with the client.

Successfully handling an objection therefore follows the pointers given for addressing negative feedback, then clarifying and confirming that we addressed the issue(s) raised successfully, then closing the item – and the sale.

Three useful things to keep in mind for successfully handling many objections are as follows:

- Make sure the intangibles are not forgotten. Peace of mind carries added value. So does building a lasting relationship with a bank and being able to count on their goodwill and good service in the future.
- Always understand our customers' risk / reward appetite and make the risk / reward equation visible to them. Many of them forget this and object on one side (e.g. 'too low a return') when it is in fact dictated by their objectives on the other side ('absolute guarantee of invested capital').
- Be mindful of our customers' total risk picture, not just the risk relating to our specific discussions. Objections may come because the client already carries a high level of risk due to health or employment issues and does not

feel comfortable adding to that extra risks in his bank dealings, even if on the surface those risks would be well justified.

3) Concept management

A good sales person will always strive to steer the sales conversation towards concept management, instead of staying at the single-issue management level. What does this mean? Single-issue management, for example, is 'savings' – discussing savings options, specific product features and benefits, addressing a clear need of the customer.

Concept management for the above example could mean 'retirement' – understanding that the customer's savings needs are driven by his desire to secure his financial future in retirement. This is a more complex need and demands more understanding, more and different product solutions, better planning.

Following the points outline earlier under 'Consumer needs', a good sales person should always understand the full needs spectrum (current and future, stated and hidden) of a prospect or customer. That should allow for taking the discussion from a single-issue basis to a concept management discussion. This would be much more beneficial to the customer and also more profitable for the bank.

Operating at the concept management level also allows for demonstrating our value added, helps address negative feedback and helps us deal with objections at the value-added level.

4) Stick with it

If you remember the concept of being a financial physician, you will not be surprised at yet another medical analogy. Unfortunately, most of us are familiar with antibiotics. Do you remember the key thing about taking them? One has to carry on taking the pills for at least one week; otherwise they have exactly the opposite effect to that desired: instead of getting rid of bacteria they will make bacteria stronger.

This is another powerful sales concept. Customers are subjected to a barrage of media messages promoting the latest theories and fads, competitive offers that look good at the first sight, scaring listeners into reckless actions, creating anxiety.

On the other hand, a good sales discussion should create a mini financial plan that needs to be followed. If a client takes a line of credit today for good reasons, it is very unlikely that things will change so dramatically tomorrow that this option should be changed. The same goes for investments and all other offers. 'Sticking with it' – keeping the course – is what is needed most of the time to realise the benefits of careful planning. We owe it to our customers to make this clear to them.

Getting the most

At the end of the day, we need to get tangible results from the time we have spent with prospects and customers. We need to justify our salary and earn our bonus. Closing the sale is one of the most difficult things for new sales people to do. Some do not feel comfortable saying "So please, sign here". Some keep on selling long after they should have stopped and may miss that 'golden moment'.

Here are some pointers to getting the most out of all the hard work we (or our staff) have put into getting to the point where we can make it happen...

1) Close!

When all the needs have been discussed and addressed, all objections handled, it is time to close the deal. Let us stop selling anymore. It is that simple.

2) Be realistic

Nobody has a 100% closure rate. It is a numbers game. The more closing opportunities we generate, the more we will close.

3) Closure is more than the sale

The best outcome is closing the sale. But closure can mean many other things. The key is never to let the time we have spent go to waste by leaving things hanging.

If we can close the sale – great. If we cannot, we must book a follow-up step. Sadly, it is my experience that most bank sales staff do not attempt to close and do not even attempt to book a follow-up. In my extensive mystery shopping experiences eight times out of 10 I have had to insist on getting the sales person's contact details for possible follow-up from my end, instead of them insisting on a next step.

If we did a good job we should also ask for a referral. ("I hope you will think that you have gained something from our discussion. I would be glad to help others with similar issues. Could you suggest some names of people I could offer the same help to?")

4) Get the technique right

Practice makes perfect. Well, maybe not, but having the technique well practiced surely helps. We need to know when to shift into 'closing mode', how to say things, how to make it easy for our prospect to say yes. Here are some specific pointers:

- Watch for signs. These signs can be verbal or non-verbal. A verbal clue could be the customer saying "Yeah, I think this would work". A non-verbal clue could be the customer reclining in his chair, smiling and nodding. Both should trigger 'closing mode'.
- Practice different closing methods. A straight-out close could happen when there is full agreement. It is that "Where do I sign?" moment. A more frequent close is the so-called 'assumptive close'. It is more like: "Okay, I will then prepare the paperwork for the loan and tomorrow at 2pm you would drop by with the salary slip to sign. I will book myself for that time right now."
- Make it easy. If the customer is hesitant, remind him of the cooling-off period (if one is offered in your market or by your bank), allowing him to change his mind with no penalty. Offer five days (or whatever may be laid down by regulators or statute) before you lock in those investments, as long as you get the funds tomorrow. There are other examples, but they all take advantage of consumer inertia. People will rarely go back and revisit a 'closed' item – it is just too time consuming for most. And, as long as we followed our needs-

based assessment model and ethical sales guidelines, they should have no reason to go back anyway.

If the customer is strapped for time, offer to have an agent visit or someone call from the call centre to finish the deal. Book a time for this, not more than two to three days away. Again, the list goes on… The basic principle remains the same though: make it easy to say yes, make it easy to take the final steps.

5) Follow up

Surprise your new (and old) customers by following up. Give a quick call and ask: "Was the mortgage disbursed right? Were you happy with how our operations team handled it?" This will earn you the right to suggest at the same time additional ideas – cross-selling and up-selling. This is one of the most powerful relationship building tools, yet hardly any sales person ever uses it.

6) Learn and refine

Nobody is perfect. Nobody will ever be. The key differentiator between successful sales people and the less successful ones is that the former keep learning. They look at what they did right, what they could have done better and use that knowledge the next time. If you are involved in active selling, do it. If you are managing a sales force, promote the idea among them. Ask the question in your sales meetings: "What could we do better?"

Closing techniques

One of the most important stages of selling is closing the deal, which is the action taken by the sales person to gain agreement to the sale. There are many closing techniques in sales, which are prescribed actions that sales people take to persuade the customer to make the necessary commitment. The website of David Straker, ChangingMinds.org, lists no less than 68 key techniques. It also has probably the best summary of sales closing techniques one can hope to find. Here is his list:

- 1-2-3 close – close with the principle of three.
- Adjournment close – give them time to think.
- Affordable close – ensuring people can afford what you are selling.
- Alternative close – offering a limited set of choices.
- Artisan close – show the skill of the designer.
- Ask-the-manager close – use manager as authority.
- Assumptive close – acting as if they are ready to decide.
- Balance-sheet close – adding up the pros and the cons.
- Best-time close – emphasise how now is the best time to buy.
- Bonus close – offer delighter to clinch the deal.
- Bracket close – make three offers – with the target in the middle.
- Calculator close – use calculator to do discount.

- Calendar close – put it in the diary.
- Companion close – sell to the person with them.
- Compliment close – flatter them into submission.
- Concession close – give them a concession in exchange for the close.
- Conditional close – link closure to resolving objections.
- Cost of ownership close – compare cost over time with competitors.
- Courtship close – woo them to the close.
- Customer-care close – the customer care manager calls later and re-opens the conversation.
- Daily cost close – reduce cost to daily amount.
- Demonstration close – show them the goods.
- Distraction close – catch them in a weak moment.
- Doubt close – show you doubt the product and let them disagree.
- Economic close – help them pay less for what they get.
- Embarrassment close – make not buying embarrassing.
- Emotion close – trigger identified emotions.
- Empathy close – empathise with them, then sell to your new friend.
- Empty-offer close – make them an empty offer that the sale fills.
- Exclusivity close – not everyone can buy this.
- Extra information close – give them more info to tip them into closure.
- Fire sale close – soiled goods, going cheap.
- Future close – close on a future date.
- Give-take close – give something, then take it away.
- Golden bridge close – make the only option attractive.
- Handover close – someone else does the final close.
- Handshake close – offer handshake to trigger automatic reciprocation.
- Humour close – relax them with humor.
- Hurry close – go fast to stop them thinking too much.
- IQ close – say how this is for intelligent people.
- Minor points close – close first on the small things.
- Never-the-best-time close – for customers who are delaying.
- No-hassle close – make it as easy as possible.
- Now-or-never close – to hurry things up.
- Opportunity cost close – show cost of not buying.

- Ownership close – act as if they own what you are selling.
- Price-promise close – promise to meet any other price.
- Puppy close – acting cute to invoke sympathy and a nurturing response.
- Quality close – sell on quality, not on price.
- Rational close – use logic and reason.
- Repetition close – repeat a closing action several times.
- Retrial close – go back to square one.
- Reversal close – act as if you do not want them to buy the product.
- Save-the-world close – buy now and help save the world.
- Selective-deafness close – respond only to what you want to hear.
- Shame close – make not buying shameful.
- Shopping list close – tick off list of their needs.
- Similarity close – bond them to a person in a story.
- Standing-room-only close – show how others are queuing up to buy.
- Summary close – tell them all the things they are going to receive.
- Testimonial close – use a happy customer to convince the new customer.
- Thermometer close – they score out of 10, you close gap.
- Think about it close – give them time to think about it.
- Treat close – persuade them to 'give themselves a treat'.
- Trial close – see if they are ready for a close.
- Ultimatum close – show negative consequences of not buying.
- Valuable customer close – offer them a special 'valued customer' deal.
- Yes-set close – get them saying 'yes' and they'll keep saying 'yes'.

With David's kind permission, we review below the main techniques, generously borrowing from his site. (If you want to learn more about them, or about other techniques that relate to persuasion, you may want to visit www.changingminds.org yourself.)

The above is a big list, but the real list of closing techniques is almost endless. You can go to each need, for example, and invent several closes around satisfying or threatening them. 'Sell on the tangibles, close on the intangibles' is good general advice. You will see how many of the following methods adhere to this rule. This is also the mirror image of the old marketing adage: 'People buy with their heart and justify their decision with their head.'

Don't forget the caveat to all of this: if people feel tricked or betrayed they will not only not buy from you now, they may never buy from you again. They may even turn all their friends against you. Usually everybody is aware of this with professional buyers, who can of course see tricks coming from miles away. Our job, as ethical sales people, is to treat every customer as one of those 'professional buyers'.

1-2-3 close

Technique

Summarise in sets of three items. We will give you this, that and the other. This may be features of the product, benefits or add-on sweetener items.

There are two ways to do this: they may either be closely related (to reinforce a single point) or may be quite separate (to gain greater coverage).

Most customers want offers that are free, perfect and available now. This is the classic 'business measurement trio' of cost, quality and time.

Examples

> *"Our unsecured line of credit is more flexible than the competition's, has a lower rate than borrowing on your credit card and has no set-up fee, unlike secured lines."*

> *"If you apply today, we promise approval within three days and give you a reduced rate balance insurance, while still guaranteeing to beat major competitors' rates."*

How it works

The 1-2-3 close works through the principle of triples, a curious pattern where three things given together act as a coherent set of three hammer-blows that give a compelling message.

Adjournment close

Technique

Do not go for the sale now. Give them time to think. Tell them that they probably need time to consider the offer you have made.

Use this when:

- You can see that they are not going to decide now;
- You have set up enough tension that you are reasonably convinced that they will indeed seriously consider the deal and are likely to come back;
- Given some more time, it is likely that they will buy more (for example if they are at the edge of a budgetary period and their current funds are low);
- The relationship is important to you, and their making a wrong decision now would affect the chances of making sales in the future;
- You do not need to make the sale today (for example, you have made your quota and this sale would be just fine for next month).

Combine this with setting up the next meeting, when perhaps you will be able to solidly close the deal.

Examples

> *"This is an important decision for you and I think you need time to consider how important it is. Shall we discuss the details further next time I see you?"*
>
> *"I can see you're thinking very carefully about this. Shall I come back next week to see how you are progressing then?"*

How it works

In many sales situations the relationship is very important as the sales person will be going back to the customer with more sales to make. It is thus a bad idea to push them into a decision when they are not ready and may later be unhappy about this.

Offering an adjournment can be a nice surprise for the customer, who may be expecting a harder style of selling. This sets up an exchange tension, encouraging them to pay back your offer of time with later agreeing to the deal.

The adjournment close is particularly easy to manage when the sales person visits the customer, as opposed to having to hope that they will call back.

Affordable close

Technique

Close out any objections they have about price/rate by making sure they can afford it.

Find how much they can afford. Then show them a payment structure that fits their capability to pay.

Bring in other factors to reframe the real price, such as lifetime costs.

Show the price of not buying – for example, the cost of continued ownership of the current car instead of buying a new one, although on credit.

Always remember the caveat: do not close people into debt they will not be able to repay.

Examples

> *"How much per month can you afford...yes, we can make that work..."*
>
> *"The initial costs seem high, but by the end of the year you will have recouped the costs by ...."*
>
> *"The cost per transaction of this account is the lowest."*

How it works

The affordable close works by structuring the deal to fit into the other person's ability to pay.

"I can't afford it" is often more of an excuse than a real objection. If they really do not want to buy, you will find that they will immediately jump onto another objection.

Alternative close

Technique

The alternative close works by offering more than one clearly defined alternative to the customer.

The number of alternatives should be very few – two or three is often quite adequate. If you offer too many alternatives, the customer will then be faced with a more complex problem of how to choose between too many alternatives.

Note that this technique works well in many different situations where you are seeking agreement, and not just selling products.

An extra technique that can be effective is to add a slight nod when offering the preferred choice. This can be accompanied by subtle verbal emphasis on the words.

Examples

> *"At the end, do you prefer the guaranteed capital or the higher yield option?"*
>
> *"So which of these three pension plans seems best to you?"*
>
> *"Shall we meet next week or the week after?"*

How it works

The alternative close is a variant on the broader-based assumptive close and works primarily through the assumption principle, where you act as if the customer has already decided to buy, and the only question left is which of a limited number of options they should choose.

Artisan close

Technique

In the artisan close, the sales person emphasises the art, skill and ability that has gone into the creation of the product or service that is being sold.

Examples

> *"The key strategist behind our emerging markets fund has 30 years' investment experience in the markets where he invests and lived in seven of them."*
>
> *"It may seem like a small difference, but it took three years of fine tuning our investment strategy to get the fund perform like this, with our new approach."*

How it works

When we are going to buy something, we evaluate it in terms of the work that went into it. If we think it was easy to make, then we value it less. Often we do not realise the effort and skill required to produce something and hence think it is worth very little.

Selling with the artisan close adds perceived value simply by describing the skill of those who made the item and the time spent in producing it.

There is a similar though slightly different approach, where the perceived value can be enhanced by explaining the training and skill of those who will be delivering the service.

Ask-the-manager / Ask-head-office close

Technique

Tell the customer that you only have limited authority to give discounts and that you will have to ask your manager to give more. You can at this point ask if the customer wants you to do this.

Then go to speak with the manager. Come back and say you have managed to persuade the manager to give an extra discount.

Examples

> *"I'm sorry, that's all the rate cut I'm allowed to give. But I've known you for a while (you are someone we'd like to have as a customer) so I'll call head office and ask, just to be sure."*
>
> *"Well, it took some persuading but I said we are nearly there so they agreed to an additional discount of a quarter percent."*

How it works

The basic principle here is that in approaching their manager, the sales person is setting up an exchange: they have put themself out for you, so you are now obliged to do something for them – like taking the offer. This is amplified as head office can be a fear-inspiring authority, thus making the salesperson a courageous warrior, fighting on behalf of the customer.

Having to ask the manager also puts a break in discounting and some people will pay the given price rather than add the hassle of the manager's intervention.

Assumptive close

Technique

Act as if the other person has made the decision already.

Turn the focus of the conversation towards the next level of questions, related to the steps to be taken after the sale.

Examples

"When would you be able to wire over the funds?"

"Which of your accounts would you like us to send the money to?"

"Can I call your guarantor to come in and sign or will you want to do it?"

How it works

The assumptive close works on the assumption principle, where acting confidently as if something is true makes it difficult for the other person to deny this. For them to say you are wrong would be to cast themselves as an antisocial naysayer.

Note: This is one of the most common closes used. Many other closes, such as the alternative close are variants of the assumptive close.

Balance-sheet close

Technique

List both the benefits of the purchase (the pros) and also the costs (the cons). Of course, the pros (the reasons to buy) will win.

You can even write it down like a balance sheet. Make sure the 'pros' column is longer and more impressive, of course.

Cons include things they wanted but are not getting. Start with the cons and keep them short. But do make it sound credible, as if you are giving them fair consideration.

Then cover the pros. Perhaps sound pleasantly surprised as you describe them.

Sound reasonable, as if you are on their side. Sound almost as if you are talking to yourself.

Example

"Let's weigh things up. You're not getting ..., but will have ..., ... and .... Hmm. That's good!"

How it works

The balance-sheet close works by building trust through appearing to taking a balanced and fair approach. It guides the other person's thinking and hopefully saves them the trouble of weighing up the pros and the cons.

This is also known as the Abraham Lincoln close (Lincoln was a lawyer and often used this technique in his cases) or the Ben Franklin close.

Best-time close

Technique

When people are procrastinating or will 'be back', emphasise how now is the best time to commit. All sales people know that 'there are no be-backs'.

This technique is easier to use in other industries, where one can invoke seasonal effects, (such a summer, Christmas and other holidays), or remind them of other short-term reasons, including sales, weather, and so on.

In financial services best-time close usually relates to limited time promotional offers or strongly competitive market seasonalities. For example, in many countries people can make tax advantageous investments before filing their income tax returns. This makes for a very competitive rate / offer situation just before filing deadlines. There is nothing wrong with acknowledging this and using it to close sales.

The good news is that (remember the 'time horizon dependence'?) today is almost always better to make a financial decision than tomorrow. Use this fact!

One strong caveat here: if you are using rate forecasts to make the 'best time' point (rates will go up / down) make sure you are using your company's approved projection and not your own. Otherwise you may be committing mis-selling and be legally liable.

Sometimes you may want to do a reversal on 'never the best time to buy' by showing how this makes now as good a time as any.

Examples

> *"The pension savings season is over next Monday. Usually deposit rates drop just when this happens. If you decide today you can still enjoy the high rates."*
>
> *"Financial decisions are best when made for the long term. The best time to start therefore is today."*
>
> *"There is no 'best time to commit' which makes now the best time."*
>
> *"If you were going to start saving money, when would you start?"*

How it works

The best-time close works by emphasising how now is the best time to buy and how delaying is not the best thing to do.

Bonus close

Technique

When they are dithering close to a decision, offer them something unexpected and un-asked for that delights them. All it needs to do is make them say "Ooh, that's nice", or something like that.

A simple equation: delight = expectation + 1

Try and figure them out before using this close: for some people it will open them up again as they seek to gain more concessions.

Examples

This is a technique that works best with physical promotions. As these are becoming ever more rare in financial services, I will skip examples here.

How it works

The bonus close may work in several ways. First, the bonus is a temptation, so that when they emotionally close on the bonus, the sensation of closure may also leak across to the main subject. Also, when they feel they have got something for nothing, they may agree to the deal for fear that you may take it away from them again.

You may also create a sense of exchange, because you have given them something.

The bonus close is also known as the delighter close or the extra close.

Bracket close

Technique

Make the other person three offers.

First, offer them something sumptuous and expensive that is beyond their budget, but not so far beyond them that they would not consider it. Ideally, it is something they would look at wistfully but just couldn't justify (if they do, it is your lucky day!).

Second, offer them a solid good deal that is within their price bracket. It may not have all that they wanted, but it is clearly good value for them.

Finally, offer a severely cut-down deal in which very little of what they want is included.

They should, of course, go for the middle option.

Examples

Again, this is a technique that is hard to make work in financial services. However, it is worth listing!

How it works

The bracket close works by contrasting the preferred option both upwards and downwards.

Rejecting the higher option lets the other person feel good about not spending too much. By comparison, the option they choose seems quite prudent and they may even feel they have saved some money.

Rejecting the lower option lets them feel they are not a cheapskate and can afford something of value.

Calculator close

Technique

Rather than just quoting a rate, get out a calculator and work the numbers into the most convincing format. This is putting the 'power of numbers' principle, discussed earlier, into action.

Example

> *"You said you can get a 0.25% better rate at bank X. However, they will charge you a 0.15% transfer fee when you get your money back. So, with this six-month deposit, one half of 0.25 is 0.125, minus 0.15, which means that you are actually losing with their higher rate against our 'lower' one..."*

How it works

Working on the calculator also implies that you are not just quoting any rate, but working out the specific circumstances for this customer. You are also performing what seems to be a difficult task with ease and exude an air of authority. Both of these invoke the exchange principle, where the customer feels more obliged to agree to the sale.

Showing the numbers also gives a finality to the action. To ask for further changes would mean you would have to recalculate and so oblige the person further.

Calendar close

Technique

If they are not ready to close now, agree a future date when you can meet to discuss further. This at least keeps the deal alive and you return to fight another day. It may also be just what you are seeking to take you to the next step in the deal strategy.

Putting dates in the diary may also be an assumptive method, assuming that closure has taken place and that it is just a matter of when.

Examples

> *"When shall we make the next meeting?"*
>
> *"Are you free next Wednesday at 3pm?"*
>
> *"What new things shall we discuss next week?"*

How it works

Putting a date in the diary is easy for the other person, and may be agreed as an exchange for you not pressing further for a close now.

Dates in the diary also get them thinking about the future, which may be a good thing as this attention will then keep them engaged in your subject-matter.

Companion close

Technique

Rather than sell directly to the person you are targeting, sell to a person they are with. This can be a husband, wife, child, friend, grandparent, etc.

Start by being friendly with them (the target person won't mind this) then gradually increase the selling to them.

Cast them as an authority (particularly as they buy into your idea).

When they are making approving noises or say they would like one, start selling to the real target of the sale.

Rope in the companion as a sales assistant.

If you are lucky, you might make two sales!

Example

I can give a personal story here as the best example. When my wife and I were discussing our pension investments at the bank we finally chose for it, they used this technique perfectly. While I was the ultimate decision-maker, as the one with financial background in the family, they quickly realised that I would not agree to anything my wife would not feel comfortable with.

So they targeted my wife with messages putting her mind at ease about how they would manage our money and gave me only 'reassurance' about the technical details (which were, in fact, the most important factors). After the meeting, my wife told me they were the only ones so far she felt comfortable with. While they were one of three companies with equally good 'technical' offers, the case was at that point decided. They won, by using the 'companion sale' approach perfectly.

How it works

The companion close usually works because the companion to whom you are selling the idea does not have to make a financial or other commitment and so might be more ready to agree with you.

When the real target of the sale sees that the other person has agreed, they are more likely to also agree, in order to maintain consistency with their thoughts of their companion being intelligent and to maintain harmony in their relationship with them.

Compliment close

Technique

Be nice to them. Tell them how wonderful they are. Be amazed and impressed by them.

Cast them as the expert so they sell to themselves.

Tell them how impressed you are with them as a person. Admire their integrity.

Then ask for the sale.

Also, compliment them on previous decisions. It does not hurt to tell them that their finances are in a very good order, considering everything – they must have thought very hard about it and made a lot of good decisions to get here.

Examples

> *"Wow. You really know your stuff. I guess I don't need to get into any more details about how our offer would be perfect for you."*
>
> *"Well, as you are obviously an expert, you will understand how good this is."*

> *"Sorry, I did not want to insult your intelligence. You probably already understand everything about our offer. Need I say more?"*

How it works

The compliment close works by flattering the other person, massaging their ego so they are more concerned with feeling good than parting with their money. It works by being nice to the other person so they feel obliged to be nice to you and take your offer.

Putting the other person on a pedestal and admiring them encourages them to live up to the high expectations you have of them. Complimenting them on a previous decision is telling them that they make good decisions (and hence can make a good decision this time too).

The compliment close is also known as the vanity close, the ego close or the flattery close.

Concession close

Technique

Offer a concession of something they want in return for them buying the product.

You can be explicit about wanting an order in return for the concession or you can give the concession without asking – the other person will very likely still feel they owe you something for it.

Examples

> *"If I reduce my commission by 25%, will that be enough for you to commit today?"*

> *"If you are ready now, I'll make sure the money is in your account by the end of tomorrow, instead of the usual three working days."*

How it works

The concession close works by offering the other person something and either requesting or implicitly expecting something in return – usually the sale.

The concession close is also called the trade-off close.

Conditional close

Technique

When the other person offers an objection, make it a condition of resolving their objection that they make the purchase.

You can also use this approach to make any trade – for example, if you want them to watch a promotional video, offer a cup of coffee.

Always, by the way, phrase it in the form 'If I...will you...' rather than 'Will you...if I...'. This is because our brains work very quickly and starting with 'will you' causes them to begin thinking immediately about objections and they may miss the exchange.

On the other hand, starting with 'If I...' will cause psychological closure on what you are offering, thus drawing them in to the close.

Examples

> *"You say you want the loan within two days. If I can phone up and get you one today, will you sign right now?"*
>
> *"If we can figure out an affordable payment structure, will fill out the paperwork with me today?"*
>
> *"If I get you a cup of coffee, would you like to sit down and look through the brochure?"*

How it works

The conditional close uses the exchange principle to build a social agreement that if I solve your problem, you will buy the product in return.

Cost of ownership close

Technique

Do not talk about price. Instead, talk about the total cost of ownership, including service, replacement, and so on.

Then compare this cost against that of competing products.

It is often good to scale this price to annual, monthly or weekly cost, where the overall cost may appear scarily high.

Example

> *"I know the other banks offered you 0.25% higher rates for these deposits. But with us you have unlimited freedom to switch your funds into one of our investment funds at any time, without fees. So you can take advantage of market changes at no cost. With the amounts we are discussing this would easily save you the equivalent of a 0.35% rate difference over the next two years."*

How it works

People often focus on the immediate price/rate and miss the longer-term costs that may be incurred if they got the same offer elsewhere. The cost of ownership close works by comparing costs of similar offers over time rather than upfront payments. If possible, this can be put into effect with staged payments.

Courtship close

Technique

Woo the other person like you were wooing a mate. Pay attention to them. Give them sincere compliments. Buy them dinner, if that is appropriate. Put them on a pedestal.

Generally treat the other person as if you like them, as a person, and that selling is a secondary issue.

If the sale is taking place over a period of time, work hard to develop the relationship. Call them often enough to show your interest. Make them welcome when they visit. Be someone who makes them feel special.

The final request for the sale is like proposing marriage to them. If they truly love you (or at least how you have been treating them), they will, of course, say yes.

Beware of harassment, stalking and other unwanted attention, of course. You want to attract them, not frighten them away.

Example

> *"Do you have time for a lunch meeting next week? I promise no business talk, I'd just like to get to know you a bit better. I actually like talking with you."*

(This is also from personal experience. I have had numerous insurance representatives and investment advisers make me these offers when considering changing insurance policies and portfolios the last time.)

How it works

This is a technique that works mostly in selling private banking services or offers with long-term relationship potential, such as insurance. Selling is very close in many ways to courtship. Or maybe it is the other way around. Whatever, the courtship close works by using many of the methods that young men use to woo young women. Or women men, or men men, or whatever. Courtship varies around the world and even around one country. So know the triggers and press the right buttons and the other person will be flattered enough to buy you, hook, line and sinker.

Customer-care close

Technique

After a meeting that does not result in a close, call up the customer as the customer service manager. Explain that it is a normal follow-up call to check the quality and customer-orientation of the sales staff.

Ask about the appearance, courtesy and knowledge levels of the sales person. This, in itself, is highly valuable information.

Then ask for reasons why they did not buy. This gives you objection information you can then address. For example, you can say that because they have been so helpful, you (as the manager) can offer an extra discount.

Examples

> *"Hello, Mr X. I'm the customer service manager at XYZ. I believe you spoke with one of our sales representatives on Monday? We have a strong customer service policy in the company and regularly check to ensure we are helping you*

at every step of the way. Could you take a couple of minutes to help answer a few questions?"

"Mr. X, I can understand why it seemed a bit out of range. However, I'd like to thank you for your help today by offering you ..."

How it works

The customer-care close shows that you care about the person, building trust and creating a bond between the customer and the service manager. It also gives you information that you can use to both improve your sales technique and also handle objections in this sale.

Daily cost close

Technique

Reduce the total cost to how much it costs per day (or week, or month). This is particularly useful for a product or service that has a limited lifetime.

Example

"Would you pay $10.50 a week for complete peace of mind? Our insurance package covers a lot for not very much."

How it works

When people estimate cost, they often do so as a single 'chunk'. By reducing the apparent cost to the smallest possible unit, the person has to do a complex calculation to work out the total cost, which many people will not bother to do. (See 'The power of numbers' earlier for reference.)

Demonstration close

Technique

If you are able to, do a spectacular demonstration of your product that really impresses them.

If you can't do it with them there (which is by far and away the best), then use a video or otherwise add impact.

Give them a go. Let them try and find out for themselves.

In financial services this technique usually involves 'test driving' different financial scenarios with the help of a spreadsheet, ideally with graphical representation of the results – instantly.

Examples

"Let me show you some charts of our investment returns over the last recession. Pretty impressive, aren't they?"

"Here is a planning programme. Let's make some assumptions about interest rates and the equity markets. Let's say ... and ... . So, as you can see, your returns would still be ... ."

How it works

The demonstration close works by giving them evidence that they cannot deny. The visceral experience of sensing a product or testing an offer with their own assumptions can never be beaten by talk.

It is particularly effective if they have already predicted that your demonstration will not work as, being forced to revise a prediction they will also have to revise the beliefs on which it was based.

Distraction close

Technique

This involves deliberately distract them or wait for a moment when they are distracted by something else, such as the kids playing up, a phone going or something like that. In other words, catch them in a weak moment when their minds are elsewhere.

Then press for the close. Ask directly for the sale. Give them the contract to sign. Warning: This is a pretty dishonest sales close approach and is not recommended. However, it can be very powerful. You should know about it if for no other reason than being able to detect it in others ... and avoiding it consciously.

Examples

(Their phone goes off). *"So you do want it now, right?"*

(There is a lot of disturbance nearby). *"Can you just quickly sign here?"*

"Here's a cup of coffee. Would you like some cake? Just sign there...that's fine."

How it works

The distraction close works by waiting until they are approaching emotional overload or have only a part of their rational mind on you. At these times, they will not be thinking quite as carefully about objecting, and agreeing to the sale will take some of the load off their minds.

Doubt close

Technique

Express doubt either about the product or the readiness of the person for the product, but make this a relatively weak and easily challenged statement.

Pause to let the person disagree, which a contradicting person will almost certainly do. If they do not challenge your doubt, then smoothly continue with a summary of everything so far.

Examples

> *"I don't know if this product is the right thing for you."*
>
> *"I'm not sure if you're ready for this. Although it does ..."* (review benefits).
>
> *"Although most people do not know how to use these, perhaps you can..."*

How it works

The doubt close works by pre-empting their doubting thoughts. If you echo these thoughts, it saves them from having to think the same thoughts. When they accept these, they will begin to trust you and hence will be ready to accept suggestions of other things to think.

Economic close

Technique

Focus on the overall economic situation, showing how the cost is less / the return is greater by considering certain factors.

Show how taking competitive offers has hidden costs.

Structure deals for them that will cost less / generate higher returns overall.

Talk about the longer-term costs or returns.

Examples

> *"Of course, you also get free fund transfers on your account with our automatic internet banking offer. So even if our rates are lower, you will be much better off overall – that's why so many people come to us from the competition."*
>
> *"If you also apply for a credit card you are eligible for our 'family pricing' on your loan too, saving you $X on a $10,000 amount over three years."*

How it works

Many people focus solely on price, and this plays directly to their concern by showing you are trying to save them money. By doing this, you also gain trust and may be able to sell them more. Even those who are not so concerned about price will have it as an issue at some level, and again you will impress them by taking up this cause for them.

Embarrassment close

Technique

Manoeuvre them into a position where not buying would embarrass them. Dissuade them from buying cheap (rather than 'less expensive') options by pointing out that they are cheap, low quality, etc. and that more expensive options are much better value.

Sell to the people they are with, so the other person would have to disappoint their friends, family, etc. by not buying.

Appeal to their sense of importance and affluence.

Examples

> *"This managed fund has the lowest upfront fee. This one, however, is much better performer."*
>
> *"Because of the large upfront amount required not many of our clients can afford this one."*

How it works

The embarrassment close appeals to emotions such as pride. It uses the alignment principle to get people to align their buying actions with their self-image of kind, affluent, etc.

It works particularly well if the other person is in a social situation where the embarrassment would be particularly strong, from a group of peers to a person of the opposite sex.

Young men, perhaps unsurprisingly, are particularly susceptible to the embarrassment close.

Emotion close

Technique

Play to their emotions, deliberately evoking specific emotions.

Find if they respond more to positive or negative emotions and act accordingly.

If in doubt, go for positive emotions – these are usually better.

Examples

> *"If you made this decision now, how would you feel?"*
>
> *"Does imagining that make you feel good?"*
>
> *"People who pass up on opportunities like this invariably feel bad later."*

How it works

The emotion close works because all decisions are based on emotions. Even if you go through a logical thought process, the final step is always emotional.

Empathy close

Technique

Empathise with them. Feel what they feel. Walk a mile in their shoes. Understand their situation completely.

Then, when they are empathising back, you decide like they would decide.

You can even talk about yourself, using 'I' instead of 'you'.

Also empathise with the product you are selling and bring this into the equation. Be a match-maker in bringing this great product to a worthy customer.

Examples

> *"I completely understand...and it makes so much sense to me to do this now."*

> *"You know, this solution works so well for me."*

How it works

The empathy close works by first harmonising yourself with them and then, when you feel what it is like for them to close, they naturally come along with you.

Done well, you will close at the exactly the right moment and for exactly the right reasons for them, and they will come back again and again.

The empathy close is also called the love close.

If you love the product you are selling and love your customers, you will be a truly great salesperson.

Empty-offer close

Technique

Make them a very kind offer that they cannot take up.

Offer to do something using a thing you have for sale, and which they might feasibly have but probably do not have.

Then sell them that thing. If they do have one, of course you must complete your offer with good grace – it will still help build social capital for you.

Examples

> *"Can I include your monthly insurance fees in this calculation? ... Oh, you have none. Well fortunately, we have some very good ones we are offering this month..."*

> *"I could probably save you half of the income protection insurance you have right now on your mortgage. Oh, you don't have one? Well, did you know you can bring your mortgage to us and get protected against job loss?"*

How it works

Although the empty-offer close does not require that you to giving them something, the rules of exchange mean that they still feel that they owe you something in return for your generous offer.

Exclusivity close

Technique

Explain how not everybody is allowed to buy this item and that some form of 'qualification' is needed.

If they do not meet the criteria, you can quietly 'let them' buy as a special favour.

Example

> *"This exchange rate is for premium clients only. I can book the transaction like it right now but I'd like to talk our premium offer through with you. I think you might qualify for it."*

How it works

When we are told we cannot have something, our sense of control is offended, so we are motivated to take control.

When we find we qualify for something, then our sense of identity is boosted as we gain a sense of belonging to a 'special group' (and which makes our satisfaction with the purchase higher).

Extra information close

Technique

When they are prevaricating, give them some additional information that will help them decide now.

If they look uncertain, and you do not have extra convincers to hand, you can ask them if they need more information.

Examples

> *"I forgot to tell you that our mortgage also has a term extension feature to let you cut your monthly payments if needed. That's hard to beat!"*

> *"Subscription to the fund may close this week. There's been quite a rush into it this week."*

> *"You look like you need more information – what else do you need to know before you decide?"*

How it works

How much information a customer needs before they decide is very variable. It is easy to overload them and scare them off, so generally it is better in the first instance to err on the side of caution. This can leave them with not enough information and this is what you may see in their hesitation to close.

It may also be that in their rationalising of your arguments and their needs, they may have reached a position where they need more information again to get to the finish line. In any case, your job is to find what they need and to give it to them so they have no reason not to buy.

Fire sale close

Technique

Explain how this is a one-off opportunity and that prices are low because of a particular circumstance beyond your control. Also point out how time-scales are limited.

Emphasise your misfortune with your manner, being down at heart rather than upbeat.

Examples

> *"The bank needs four-month money, so we are offering a special high deposit rate for four months, this week only."*
>
> *"We have a partnership deal with IKEA and we need to sign up more customers for this credit card. So we are waiving our usual fees on applications received before next Wednesday."*

How it works

In a real fire sale, goods are variously damaged and sold off at knock-down prices to make what little you can from the damage (the alternative is to scrap them). Other things can damage goods, such as storms and floods.

In a fire sale the buyer also feels they have the upper hand as the seller is disadvantaged.

Future close

Technique

If they are not ready to close today, then close on a future date.

Perhaps they want to think it over. Ask how much time they need. Ask if they may be ready to buy then. After thinking about this, they may be ready to close now. If not, do a calendar close so you can meet up next time.

Examples

> *"How much time do you need to think about it? ... As you consider having thought about it now, what do you think?"*
>
> *"When you have thought about it, do you think you may be ready to sign?"*
>
> *"When we meet next week, will you have thought it through then?"*

How it works

The future close works by getting them to think in the present about the future, hence bringing the future to now so they can 'compress time' and possibly close now.

Give-take close

Technique

Offer them something attractive, then retract the offer, taking it away.

Then make them work to get it back. You might find they're desperate enough to pay full price.

Example

It is very hard to see how this technique could work in a financial services situation. Nevertheless, it is useful to be aware of it.

How it works

When a person sees something desirable, they start to psychologically close on it. Even paying attention creates a weak sense of ownership. When you take the product away, you affect the person's need for a sense of control with the result that they will likely fight back, figuratively trying to take back what is 'theirs'.

The scarcity principle says that people want what is scarce, and the more scarce it is, the more they want it.

Golden bridge close

Technique

If you want a person to take a particular option, do not mention it directly, but show how all other options are not feasible or undesirable.

Then let them choose the option themselves.

Example

> *"Oops, sorry, that rate is only available for balances above 10,000. And that money market fund had some bad reviews, I would not recommend it. Luckily, this term deposit looks pretty good..."*

How it works

Sun Tzu, the famous Chinese General who wrote the classic text about winning wars without fighting, said "Build your enemies a golden bridge." By this he meant you corner them, and then rather than fighting (when they, having nothing to lose, would fight to the death), you back off a little and let them leave with dignity – but in the direction you want them to go.

The golden bridge close thus works by closing off all options except the one you want.

Handover close

Technique

When you are getting near to closure or if you are having problems, hand over the actual closure to another person.

You can frame this as a different process, for example where your job was to help the customer choose and the next person is to agree final details, agree price or just take down details.

Examples

> *"Right. Now that we've got the fit right, Mr. Jones here is going to help sort out the paperwork."*

> *"You have said that price is important to you and Mrs Williams is our senior manager and is going to take over now."*

How it works

When the new person takes over, they may act as if everything else has been agreed. The new person is not encumbered with any baggage and the customer may be reluctant to go over any previous detail and effectively give in when faced with a person who may not understand objections raised.

There is a danger, of course, that the buyer will go backwards to re-negotiate detail already agreed. Other problems can also occur, such as the customer backing out because they have bonded with the initial sales person. This method must therefore be used with care.

This process can be used when junior people are used to explain the details of a product while a senior person takes over the price negotiations. Equally, it is useful when regulations or lack of knowledge prevents some staff from closing sales but they are well qualified to lead up to the closure point.

Handshake close

Technique

As you make a closing offer, extend your hand for a handshake. Smile and nod as if the deal is done. Look expectantly. If necessary, raise your eyebrows slightly.

Examples

> (Extending hand) *"So, are you ready now to do the deal today?"*

> (Extending hand) *"We have a deal?"*

> (Grasp their hand) *"Well done. You've got a good deal today."*

How it works

When you offer your hand to somebody in greeting they will automatically feel obliged to shake your hand in return, often doing this without really thinking.

When they do shake your hand, they may realise that they are also agreeing to the close. Most people will not then feel able to retract their agreement.

Humour close

Technique

Get them amused by telling a joke or otherwise making witty remarks. Then either go for a relaxed close with another closing technique or weave closure into the joke. This is particularly useful when they are tense for some reason.

Beware of politically-incorrect humour unless you are sure it will be effective.

Self-deprecating humour is often a safe bet and shows you to be confident and likable.

Examples

> *"Oh go on. It'll make both our wives very happy."*
>
> *"If you don't sign today, I'll be told to go and stand in the corner!"*
>
> *"I'd better look like you've already agreed in case the boss sees me."*

How it works

Relaxed and happy people are less likely to object.

When you make someone laugh, they will like you more. And we are more likely to buy from people we like.

Hurry close

Technique

Hurry them up. Speed up the proceedings.

Talk fast, move fast. Encourage them to do the same.

Hint (every so gently) that slower thinking is not very clever.

Say that if they cannot decide quickly then others might get the deal.

Examples

Many examples exist but as this is also a pretty dishonest technique, I will not encourage any reader to use it by giving specific details… And I hope you agree!

How it works

Speeding people up stops them from pausing to think about the reasons why they should not buy.

IQ close

Technique

Imply that intelligent people say yes to this.

This is particularly useful in selling complex offers to people who may shy away from complexity.

The intelligence can also be associated just with doing a good deal.

Examples

> *"This fund is the most popular with my doctor clients."*
>
> *"This is a really clever solution."*
>
> *"It's a bit complex, but you look like you can handle that sort of thing."*

How it works

The IQ close works by associating intelligence with closure. Thus, if people think they are intelligent (and we all do) they will be attracted towards purchasing the product and hence feel that they are intelligent.

Minor points close

Technique

Ask them about minor points, getting decisions on things they might consider if they were really going to buy the product. Then go for the final close on the offer.

Examples

> *"Would you like your picture on your credit card or not?"*
>
> *"Which card design would you choose?"*
>
> *"Do you use the internet at home? Great, that will make it easy to use our free internet banking package."*

How it works

The customer knows they need to decide on many factors, and this complexity of decision may be holding them back. By getting the easier decisions out of the way, this greatly simplifies the final decision.

After several closures on minor points, the customer gets accustomed to the pleasure of feeling of closure. They can continue this by making the purchase.

Never-the-best-time close

Technique

When people are procrastinating or dithering over whether they should buy now or buy later, show them that delaying will either get them no advantage or may even be to their disadvantage.

Talk about what they will miss by not having it over the coming period.

Give examples of people who waited for the best moment, which never came.

Examples

> *"If you leave investing until next year, you'll have one year less to earn a return on it."*

> *"My friend spent his whole life looking for the perfect partner."*
>
> *"Even the pros cannot time market entry perfectly. I always say 'just do it and sleep well'."*

How it works

The never-the-best-time close works by reframing delaying tactics as value-destroying procrastination.

No-hassle close

Technique

Make completing the deal so completely easy for them that any thought that might put them off is not there.

Fill in all forms for them. Do all the paperwork.

Include sample calculations, offer to handle funds transfers, account transfers, etc from other banks.

Examples

> *"I've filled in all the paperwork and all you need is to sign here."*
>
> *"Everything will be done by Tuesday, you don't need to do a thing. I will call you to confirm that everything went OK."*

How it works

The no-hassle close works by being so simple and easy for the other person that any anticipated difficulty or hassle that may be holding them back is blown away.

It also encourages them to return the favour as an exchange for your help with the completion.

Now-or-never close

Technique

Make them an offer, but make it short-term to the point that they must choose to buy now. Thus they cannot come back tomorrow, when the price will be higher.

Show how this is the last day of the offer.

Say that you need to make your numbers by tomorrow so you are decreasing the price more than you would otherwise.

Examples

As with most 'hurry'-type techniques, this is one I personally do not recommend. It would not work on me, so why would I subject others to it? However, as with some of the other techniques, it is included here for the sake of completeness.

How it works

The now-or-never close works by hurrying them up with a one-off deal. With less time to reflect or seek alternatives, they have to choose, and the thought of losing out will push them towards deciding now.

Opportunity cost close

Technique

Highlight the cost of not buying and hence show that the actual cost is not as high as appears from the price.

Use 'cost' in its broadest sense, including hassle, dissatisfaction and problems. Time, in particular, always costs.

Example

> *"Of course, you can save money by not taking the life insurance option with your mortgage. But can you imagine the cost to your family if, by chance, something happens to you and they cannot pay the mortgage?"*

How it works

There is always cost, whether you do or do not do something. In business and finance, the 'opportunity cost' is the name given to the cost of not doing something.

Price is not the same as cost. Price is what the customer pays in cash. Cost is a whole range of problems that may or may not be translatable into money. Cost is the sales person's friend.

Ownership close

Technique

Act as if they already own what is being sold.

Talk about 'your' product and what they are going to do with it. Discuss how it already fits into their lives. Admire it.

Do not talk about whether they are ready to buy or have already bought it. Just act as if it has always been theirs.

Example

> *"Well, I think I've explained it in great detail. So how do you like your new flexible mortgage loan?"*

How it works

The ownership close uses the assumption principle, acting as if they already owned the product. This seeks to create mental closure on the principle of already owning it.

Price-promise close

Technique

Promise to match a better rate if they find it anywhere.

Put boundaries on the offer, for example 'within the next week', 'internet offers not valid'.

Example

> *"I am so confident that we have the best rate, that if you find a better anywhere by next week I will match it – no matter what the bank says!"*

How it works

Many people fear finding a better offer somewhere else afterwards, so they are afraid to commit. The price-promise close eliminates this fear.

In practice, extremely few people take up on this type of offer, because the difference is small, they are embarrassed to ask for 'money back' or the confidence it gives them actually stops them from looking at other rates.

Puppy close

Technique

There are a number of variants of the puppy close.

Give them the product to try out. If possible let them take it home. Like a puppy, it should sell itself.

Be charming and cute, just like a puppy dog.

Flatter them. Be very nice. Act something like a good child who deserves a reward.

Another variant is to frame what you are selling in the same cute and fluffy light.

Examples

This is a technique that only works with tangible offers (products) and not really in financial services. It is included for the sake of completeness.

How it works

The puppy close, when you give them the item to try out, works by the investment principle, where as they spend time with it they grow closer to it as they associate their identity with it.

The puppy close, when you are acting in a cute way, works by appeal principle, where you appeal to their kind and gentle nature. By framing the other person as good and kind (with which, of course, they agree), you also invoke the consistency principle, where they then feel obliged to act in alignment with the way you have described them (and they have accepted as an accurate and true description).

Acting in a child role is playing the parent-child game from transactional analysis. Where you act as a needy and deserving child, you invoke the nurturing parent in them.

Quality close

Technique

Emphasise quality over other factors, particularly rates.

Sell on quality, not on price.

Examples

> *"And if you open an account with us, you will have 24-hour access to it not only by internet, but also on the phone, being able to talk to a real person whenever you want!"*

> *"If you buy our premium client package, you will have your own dedicated customer service representative and a different phone banking number than others."*

How it works

The quality close works by appealing either to the other person's vanity or to their sense of longer-term value. For vanity, you are associating their identity with 'quality'. For value, you are reframing price across time.

Rational close

Technique

Use logic and reason to persuade. Show them evidence that the product works well and that other customers were satisfied. Leverage documented cases and statistics as irrefutable proof. Explain reasonably why buying is the right choice.

With care, you can construct a powerful argument that uses a traditional and proven structure for persuasion.

Examples

> *"Well now, we've gone through all your needs and the product meets these well, right? ... And the rate is good, true? ... Now is there anything else that would stop you investing today? ... No? So let's do the paperwork."*

> *"97% of our clients said they were very happy with the flexibility of this kind of loan when we asked them six months after taking it. You can't argue with that."*

How it works

This approach works simply by using rational reasoning that calls upon logic and science. As we are brought up in a social and educational system that defines numbers and reason to be correct, such an approach is powerfully persuasive.

Some people decide by thinking and others more by feeling. This approach works well with many people, though it is most effective with the thinking decision-makers.

Repetition close

Technique

Achieve the close by repeating a closing action several times. Show them the offer, then other offers, then come back to the offer, ... and repeat this three or four times.

Tell them several reasons why they should agree.

Ask several questions that remind them about the offer.

Tell them about several different other people who took this offer.

If they refuse, go back to the offer again.

Examples

> *"Look at this...you could consider that... and this is good too... and another... I know you're not going to agree right now, but I just want to show you one more thing..."*

How it works

The repetition close works because many people need to repeat things a few times before they 'get it'. In a shoe shop, for example, they may have to pick up and put down a pair of shoes three times before they decide to buy. Imagine how much more complicated this may be when it comes to money!

Many people have a certain number of times they need to repeat things before they achieve personal closure. If you can find this number (often around three or four), then you know how many times to repeat your close.

Repetition is a very fundamental pattern that affects us in primal ways.

Retrial close

Technique

When things are not going your way, and perhaps when your customer has already said 'no' (and perhaps a number of times), then seek to reset the clock by obviating any past decisions through new data or proving that decisions were shaky or incorrect.

Examples

> *"I have looked deeper into this and found that we were using the wrong information."*
>
> *"I'm sorry but I lost my notes from last time. Can we go over a few things again?"*
>
> *"After talking with Jan, it seems the requirements have changed..."*

How it works

The retrial close works in the same way that a retrial is forced in a court of law, where evidence that was accepted in the original trial is proved to be unsafe.

Perhaps it seems it is not so much a closing technique as an unclosing technique? The actual closure is in the decision to open the negotiations again.

Reversal close

Technique

Act as if you do not want them to buy the product.

When they are objecting, just take the product back and put it on the shelf (or worse, give it to another sales person).

Suddenly remember that this is the last one and it was reserved by someone else.

When they object to you 'deciding for them', do not give in easily. Let yourself be persuaded by them, and only take the product out again when you have a much firmer interest or commitment.

This is particularly useful if they seem to have a contrary nature.

How strongly you do this reversal depends on how much they pull back. It's a bit like fishing – too much tugging and the fish will swim away, while a delicate touch will bring the fish inevitably to the shore.

You can also use the idea of reversal in other ways, for example to elicit objections by asking them why they would not buy from you.

Examples

Once again, not a technique that can work or would be recommended in financial services... but good to know about!

How it works

The reversal close works by causing reactance, where your autonomous actions cause them to take an opposite stance.

It can also be useful when they are suspicious of you trying to sell them something. By refusing to sell, you appear to be on their side or, at the very least, you will have broken their stereotype of a typical sales person.

Save-the-world close

Technique

Suggest that if they do what you ask, this will somehow lead to a significantly bigger gain being made.

Use phrasing such as "If you...then..." to show causal connection.

Example

"A small amount saved each day will give you a life of luxury in retirement."

How it works

People generally are persuaded when a causal connection between two things is stated, even though it may be tenuous.

We all like to dream and the thought of somehow achieving these dreams with relatively little effort is very attractive.

Selective-deafness close

Technique

You ignore anything that the other person says or does that does not lead you towards a close. Well, not so much ignore it as act as if it had not been said (you actually think hard about why they are saying what they do and seek ways to lead them away from it).

Examples

> (They say the rate is too high) – *"Won't it be great to have the flexibility it offers?"*
>
> (They start to walk away) – *"Just look at this feature!"*
>
> (They ask about things you do not have) – *"Would you like a cup of coffee?"*

How it works

The selective-deafness close works by the principle that you get what you talk about. If their attention is on why they cannot buy, then they are likely to not buy.

It also is related to the locus of control. If you are talking about what they want, you are on their agenda and they are in control. What you want is for them to think that they are in control, but they are actually walking down the path you control.

Shame close

Technique

Make them ashamed of the current product they have or their inaction over not buying.

Show how unfashionable they are and how others may laugh at them.

Frame not buying as 'stingy' and miserly.

Highlight other social rules that they are breaking.

Examples

> *"Can you do mobile banking with your current bank?"*
>
> *"Do you get an SMS warning about each credit card transaction from your current car provider?"*

How it works

The shame close works by highlighting social rules that the person is breaking. It also may work by appealing to their vanity.

The shame close is also called the guilt close.

Shopping list close

Technique

First elicit the buyer's needs, including product features and other elements such as service levels, usability and so on.

Write these down and verify with the buyer that this is what they want. Of course, ensure that what you write down is something that you can supply.

Then show the customer the items on the list. The 'shopping list' close is done as you check off each item as you show it.

If you can't cover everything, make sure the things you can't cover are (a) few, and (b) relatively unimportant.

Warning: Somewhat dishonest practice. 'Needs-based selling' dictates that the shopping list be complete and not partial...

Example

> *"OK. So you want a credit card that offers CDW, % back and 45-day pay period. Check, check, check!"*

How it works

The shopping list close works first by convincing the buyer that the list itself is all that they need, which is done by careful questioning and writing in a form where the seller can demonstrate compliance.

The convincing part of the close is in the way that you check off each item. The effect is that each time you do this, it causes the buyer to experience a psychological close. The repetition is like a series of hammer-blows that create a strong final close.

The completed list is also means that the buyer cannot have any objections.

Similarity close

Technique

Tell a story about a person who is 'just like' the target customer, with similar problems and concerns and who bought what you are selling and is now very happy.

Make sure the customer will empathise with the person in the story. Also be subtle – do not make the person in the story too similar. Where possible, use a real person and a real story.

Example

> *"You know I had a customer yesterday who asked the same question and who was also concerned about the effect of rate increases. I told her about the same 'rate tracker' option I just mentioned to you and she came back this morning to invest a hundred grand in it."*

How it works

When we read stories or watch movies, we associate with the protagonists and others in the story, taking on a part of their character into our selves. We thus bond with fictional characters and easily do so with people in real life (how often have you empathised with people on the news?).

Once attached to the person in the story, the customer will then more likely agree with what the character thinks and does and may well follow suit with similar decisions.

Standing-room-only close

Technique

Show how other people are all queuing up to buy the product / sign up.

Indicate that the other people are known to or are like the other person.

Hint at how they may be left behind by others or even seen as slow and backward by not buying the product sooner.

Combine it with hints of scarcity, showing how the product is so popular you may run out soon.

Examples

> *"I had six clients yesterday with similar questions to yours and every one of them took advantage of this offer!"*

> *"I don't know how many more people will be here tomorrow."*

How it works

The standing-room-only close works by the evidence principle, where the evidence of other people's interest in the product socialises it.

It shows that the person is not an early adopter but runs the danger of being in the late majority or even seen as a laggard.

Summary close

Technique

Summarise the list of benefits that the other person will receive, telling them the full extent of what they are getting for their money.

Make it sound impressive, using attractive words. Go into detail, separating out as many sub-items and features as you can.

But also fit the description into a reasonable space of time. Your goal is to impress them with what they are getting, not to bore them with excessive detail.

Example

> *"So on top of the basic offer, you are getting free internet banking, free funds transfers for a year and a 50% cut on the second credit card for your wife."*

How it works

The summary close works by repeating what has already been agreed. Putting it all together makes it seem like an even bigger package.

Testimonial close

Technique

Use a happy customer to convince the other person.

Show them letters from happy customers. Have the letters on the wall.

If you are using the name of the happy customer, make sure they agree to you doing this. Otherwise you will have to use an anonymous reference, such as 'satisfied customer from Birmingham' or 'major airline'.

Persuade happy customers to act as references that the other person can call up. Reward the happy customer with appropriate thanks, which may range from a simple letter to a small present to a discount. Be very careful here to ensure the customer feels valued and does not feel they are being bribed.

Examples

> *"I regularly receive letters from happy customers. Here are a couple."*
>
> *"XYZ Corporation is a regular customer."*
>
> *"We have several customers who are happy to act as reference sites for us. Would you like me to arrange a call for you?"*

How it works

The testimonial close works by providing evidence from a credible source. If they do not trust you, they are much more likely to trust someone who is similar to them.

Thermometer close

Technique / example / how it works

This is what I would call an upfront closing technique. By using the technique the salesperson is not trying to close the sale out but merely attempting to move the conversation and the opportunity forward.

It goes like this:

> Salesperson: "Good morning [prospect], this is [salesperson]. How are you today?"

Next the stall:

> Prospect: "Oh hi. I'm good, unfortunately I haven't made a decision yet so perhaps if you could leave it till next week that would be great."

Here comes the upfront closing technique, which allows the salesperson to test where the sale is relative to a successful close.

> Salesperson: "No problem, I will put you down for a call on Tuesday. Obviously, [prospect] I would like it be a 'yes' on Tuesday but if I were to ask you say on a scale of one to ten, ten being we definitely will be doing business and one being we definitely won't be doing business, where would you say you are right now?"

Depending on the number, the salesperson knows how much convincing is left to do. An answer of five or lower means lots and an answer of six or higher means not so much.

> Prospect: "Oh I'd say a seven or eight."

This is good, but there are still some issues/objections remaining, so next the salesperson needs to find out what these concerns are.

> Salesperson: "Great, can you tell me what are the concerns that remain or how might I help to get you to ten?"

> Prospect: "Well, really the concern relates to delivery times, and while you may have a more cost-effective solution, our current supplier never misses a deadline so we feel there is an element of risk involved."

Now the salesperson has found out the remaining concern(s) and has an opportunity to do something about that.

> Salesperson: Thanks [prospect] for your honesty and I appreciate and understand your position. How about to help you resolve this concern, I set up a call between you and one or two of our major and long-standing customers? You can ask them how we have performed in relation to meeting their deadlines."

> Prospect: "Yeah, for sure that would help."

> Salesperson: "OK, I'll speak to them immediately and set up the calls before the weekend. That should leave you with enough time to consider what's been said before our call on Tuesday. Does that sound reasonable to you [prospect]?"

> Prospect: "Yeah, that sounds good, I'll look forward to speaking to them."

Try the thermometer close for yourself. Remember, it's most effective in situations where the opportunity is stalled or when the prospect is not forthcoming with concerns or issues that they still may have.

Think about it close

Technique

After you've said what you can, give the person a little time to think about what you have told and shown them.

Don't leave them for too long (a couple of minutes is often enough) and preferably go where you can keep an eye on them. A way of handling this is to ask them how long they need.

When you return, watch their body language to see if they are showing signs of being ready to buy. If necessary, use an assumptive method to nudge them over the edge.

Examples

> *"I can see you're carefully thinking about. I'm going to step outside for a couple of minutes so you can decide in your own time."*

> *"How long would you like to think about it? Can I get you a cup of coffee while you decide?"*

How it works

Not everyone decides quickly, and if pressed many will back away or react against the sales methods being used.

Decision-making is often a complex thought process. Pros and cons are weighed up and the person may not decide until they have gone through this process. This is particularly common in sales which involve significant money or other commitment.

Sometimes it just takes a little time to sink in. You have given them a lot of information which they need to process and fit in with their current models of the world.

Of course there is a danger when the person thinks about it that they will say no. Depending on the sales context this could a bad or good thing. People who buy only because they are pressured are unlikely to return or recommend you. On the other hand, this final 'soft sell' stage may well convince them that it is they who are in control and so will make the decision to buy.

The think about it close is in some ways a form of assumptive close, as you are assuming that all they need is time to decide.

Treat close

Technique

If you are selling something that you know they would like but cannot justify to themselves that they should buy it, then persuade them that they deserve a treat.

Point out how hard they have worked and that this would be a good reward.

Find out if they have given things to others. Point out that they need to be good to themselves as well.

Give them the excuse they need. Give them a reason they can tell themselves why it is a good thing to buy now.

Examples

> *"You have worked hard all your life. Don't you think you deserve that platinum card by now?"*

> *"Look at all the things you have done for other people. Don't you think it's time to do something for yourself?"*

How it works

The treat close evokes the need for fair play, showing the other person as needing something to make up for other things they have done. It leverages the exchange principle with the other person as the deserving recipient.

Trial close

Technique

A trial close is not a normal closing technique but a test to determine whether the person is ready to close.

Use it after a presentation or after you have made a strong selling point. Use it when you have answered objections.

The trial close may use other closing techniques or may be a more tentative question.

Ask 'If...' questions.

Ask questions that assume they have already bought the product.

After you have asked the trial close question, as with most other closes, be quiet.

Watch and listen carefully for their response.

'ABC' is a common abbreviation: 'always be closing'. It means that you should always be heading towards a close, although you must also be careful about overdoing this. If people are nowhere near ready to buy, this will just annoy them.

Examples

> *"It looks like you really like this. Is that true?"*

> *"If you took the loan today, would you be proud to own new car by tomorrow?"*

> *"If you signed right now, how would you feel about it?"*

How it works

The trial close works by putting the idea of closure into the person's mind. Their response will tell you whether they are ready or not.

Ultimatum close

Technique

Show that if they do not agree to the deal now, then there will be significant negative consequences.

The most common structure for this is "If...then..."

You may be the person who implements those consequences. You may also be the friend who warns them of the consequences that they may not have realised.

Examples

> *"If you don't sign now, I'll have to talk to your manager."*
>
> *"Don't forget: this is the last day of the sale."*
>
> *"If you sign today, you will sustain your no-claims bonus. If you leave it until tomorrow, you'll have to start all over again."*

How it works

This can be a very negative method, in that it is based on threats and fear, although the threat may be cloaked in a veil of friendship.

The ultimatum, when it comes from somewhere else, may indeed be real, in that you and they have no control over whether it happens or not.

It would seem that this kind of close is not a good idea, yet it is surprisingly common, especially in one-off selling.

My personal comment is that this method would never work with me and anyone trying it would be blacklisted for life. Now, if you still want to try it...

Valuable customer close

Technique

Many would say that this technique means you have to find a reason to show that the customer is of particular value to you, and then offer them a special, one-off discount.

Or call back later as sales manager and say the customer is so valuable, you are able to offer an extra discount.

Ethical sales principles, however, say that you should use this technique only if you truly find the customer / prospect valuable. In that case, you can offer special rates and fees, or other inducements, to reward family holdings, potential business accounts, referrals and the like.

Examples

> *"You run one of the busier law practices in the area. I tell you what: I give you our best 'preferred customer' rate and promise the best service for all your clients. All I'm asking for is that you mention my name and give them my card when they ask for recommendations on financial matters."*

"I know you have your own company and I would like your company accounts too. If you would consider it, I will give you our best discretionary rates for both your personal and business funds."

How it works

The valuable customer close works by flattering the customer into believing that the discount that you are offering is more than they would normally get, and hence offers unusually good value.

Yes-set close

Technique

Ask them several questions where the answer is easy to give and is 'yes'. Then tag on the question at the end for which you really want the answer 'yes'.

The minimum set is usually three questions. You also do not want to over-do this, so either space out the questions or limit the number (although one research showed that eight yeses were needed overall before closure).

Encourage them to say yes by nodding your head gently as you talk with them.

If you need to hide the question, you can bury it among other questions.

Examples

"Would you like the 0.5% bonus rate on six months?"

"How about the full redeemability feature at no cost?"

"And you said you have the funds available?"

"So, are we ready to do the paperwork then?"

How it works

The yes-set close works by setting up a repetitive pattern of 'yes' answers that gets the other person into a habitual response. When the pattern is established and they are automatically answering 'yes', then the question that you really want 'yes' to is slipped in.

Many people also do not particularly like to answer 'no' as they believe that it is impolite.

Recap

In conclusion, I hope that this chapter gives the basic pointers on personal needs-based, consultative selling techniques. The focus has been on needs assessment, ethical selling and efficient and effective personal techniques. That is, not on the best sales management practices to operationalise and manage the process, not on structures, organisations or meetings – but on very personal approaches to be the best.

Table 2.8 attempts to summarise the most salient points. The next chapter reviews how these practices fit into sales process and sales management set-ups, and how they are used by some of the best banks in the world

Table 2.8: Needs-based personal selling – main-points

- Sell in person, service remotely
- Sell the service / product, build the relationship:

Explore	➔	Need	Ask questions
Offer	➔	Solution	Define financial need
Handle	➔	Objections	Negatives, rejections
Sell	➔	Product	Tell how our offer will help
Close	➔	Sale	Offer, follow up, referral
Service	➔	Customer	It does not end at the end of the first sales session
Build	➔	Relationship	Cross sell, up-sell, trust

- Remember:
  - We are "Financial Physicians" - need to know the problem before prescribing cure
  - The customer's problem is my problem and my *opportunity*

Source: 3-i Inc.

Chapter 3

Global best practices – overview

If you are operating in a 'standard banking environment', and have read the previous chapters, this chapter will either bore you to tears or will be the most important one for you to read. I hope it will be the latter.

We will review the essence of global best practices in a standard retail banking environment, with a great deal of detail and actual results from specific case studies of implementing these practices. By 'standard banking environment' I mean a solid multi-channel set-up, with a good range of products and reasonable trained sales force. This environment would not include, for example, branch agents but may include 'mobile bankers' (direct sales agents, or DSAs) which are far more common in retail banking today.

To make everything easy to digest I have deliberately chosen a looser style, taking advantage of many charts to illustrate key points. So, if you want to get a quick overview of best practices and efficiency benchmarks, fast, start here!

Let's start with what I consider to be globally the best sales practices of leading banks.

'No-one is afraid of selling'

First, sales staff are not afraid of selling. This should sound pretty obvious, but in many emerging markets in the world (as well as in some more advanced continental European ones) 'selling' is still regarded as a dirty word. Selling is associated with shoving something down someone's throat that they did not really want in the first place. This could not be further from the truth. In reality, selling is a higher level of service. Good sales people understand this. If yours don't, then it is up to you / us to bring them to this realisation.

What could be more satisfying than understanding the true needs of someone and offering solutions to satisfy them? That is what (good) sales is all about.

A personal anecdote here, as it relates to cross-selling: some time ago I bought a remote-control toy car for my godson. What I did not know, and had no time to check during the pre-Christmas rush, was that the toy came without batteries. Now, it is easy to blame the customer for not being aware of even such a simple thing as 'batteries not included', but the customer probably have has hundreds of other things on his mind. In the words of Cohen Brown, one of the best sales consultant companies in the world: "It is never the customer's responsibility to know anything, understand anything or have any questions ready about the services you sell."

Back to my story: the sales person in the store was either not trained in the art of cross-selling or did not want to push me to buy extra items. So he never asked me if I wanted batteries with the toy. You can imagine what happened. You can imagine my godson opening the present, his face lighting up, then realising that it would not work because there were no batteries in it. On top of that, all stores were closed for Christmas, so he could not try his new toy until the festive season was over.

Do you think I would have liked that sales person to suggest batteries (and back-up batteries too, as my five-year old godson surely would have used up the first set in the first day)? A definite 'yes' to that question. I would have liked him to think about my needs and proactively offer a solution. This would definitely have qualified as 'sales as a higher level of service'. More positive stories are in Chapter 2, where I discussed some first-rate sales behaviour I encountered recently and how they illustrate the best in personal, consultative selling.

'Everyone sells'

That's right. And not only in the sense of supporting the actual sales activity of the dedicated sales force. Sales officers are of course expected to sell proactively. But tellers / cashiers can also hand out sales brochures and cross-refer people. It takes one second to do so and generates useful leads. Of course, no call to a call centre should go without a sales attempt at the end, trying to generate interest or permission for a follow-up sales call.

Table 3.1: Sales basics of the best – 1

- **'Sales is a higher level of service' – no 'fear of selling'**
- ***EVERYBODY* SELLS:**
  - **Sales**
    - Sales Officers – active selling
    - Tellers – cross-refer, hand out brochures
    - Outreach Sales – cross-refer to branches, follow up on branch leads
  - **Marketing**
    - Direct acquisition
    - Local sales programmes
    - Marketing campaigns take into account tellers, outreach sales force, call centre, etc
  - **Credit**
    - Target segment definition for lending product
  - **Operations**
    - Flawless service quality
    - Referrals for sales follow-up
    - Call centres
  - **And more...**

Source: 3-i Inc.

'Everything is process-driven and focuses on building profit'

First, roles and responsibilities for the different channels are well defined and clearly differentiated. Customer service is best done remotely, in the least expensive way. Customer acquisition is best done in a direct fashion (DSAs, direct response advertising, etc) to drive large volumes of new contacts and fresh customers to the bank. Building relationships, however, is usually best done in person, in a branded bank environment – the branches.

The driving force behind this design is the profitability mantra of the best companies and can be summarised as follows: "Every customer, every product, every channel must be profitable on a going basis." 'On a going basis' means that loss-leader hook-offers are okay, but they should not be extended for long periods of time. We must decide the most efficient way of doing things and split activities among the different channels for the greatest efficiency.

To embed this approach, the best companies make it part of their everyday processes. In other words, they operationalise them. Nobody should be unsure about what is expected of them. When people know what they need to do, what their responsibilities and flexibilities are to deliver results, then results will happen.

I have yet to meet someone who went to work in the morning thinking: "I really want to do a bad job today." That would go against human nature. Most people want to do a good job. It is the lack of clear processes and definitions that create confusion and diminish results, not lack of motivation. Of course, if confusion lasts long enough a decline in motivation is bound to follow. All the more reason to operationalise best practices fast, before lack of clarity creates people issues over motivation. Those are much more difficult to fix…

Table 3.2: Sales basics of the best – 2

- **Highly efficient process design**
  - Acquire directly
  - Service remotely
  - Build relationship in person
- **Every channel, every customer, every product must be profitable**
- **Every customer contact is turned into proactive sales opportunity**
  -> "Have you heard about our... ?" (à la "Would you like fries with that?...")
- **To guarantee company-wide success**
  - Disciplined processes
  - Templated approach
  - Everything is 'operationalised'

"Nobody ever gets up in the morning wanting to do a really bad job today"

Source: 3-i Inc.

'Branch staff have a clear focus on cross-selling and service quality and a plan to deliver them'

It follows from what was said previously that branch staff should focus on two things:

- Building relationships with customers; and
- Providing superior service quality (which will accomplish the same thing).

Relationship building relies a great deal on discovering customers' needs they may or may not be aware of and offering solutions to them. This is simply cross-selling.

Having a plan to do it right is dealt with in great detail in the previous chapter. A key concept, worth repeating, is planning everything based on leading indicators and conversion efficiency ratios. 'Leading indicators' track the specific activities each sales person planned for himself, in order to generate enough leads for the next sales step. These include things like the number of calls per day and referrals per day, leading to sales meetings booked, etc.

Conversion efficiencies deal with how effectively each activity translates into the next one. What percentage of my calls got someone on the line? What percentage of people I talked to I could book for a personal meeting? What percentage of my meetings result in an actual sale?

Following these two items allows sales management to predict what results would be at the end of any measuring period, at any time during that period. One has truly planned one's way to success.

Just as importantly, following these indicators allows management to pinpoint any issues with quality of lists, time allocation, sales skills, etc. They can then take preventive measures – ask for different selection criteria for the call lists, reallocate capacity, coach in phone skills, to name just a few. This allows them to fix problems before they have a major impact on results and walk the path of continuous improvement.

Table 3.3: Building relationships in person

- **Dual focus for branches**
  - Cross-selling
  - Service quality
- **When done well, good results are *inevitable***
- **To guarantee personal success**
  - Use leading indicators: number of calls, number of meetings, etc and
  - Efficiency ratios: % of calls turned into meetings, % of meetings ending in sales, ...
- **You should know whether you will reach your month-end goals every day of the month**

Source: 3-i Inc.

Providing superior customer service quality is also a key requirement for branch staff. There are numerous studies and calculations showing why this should be so. The following tables attempt to summarise the key facts about cross-selling and customer service quality.

Table 3.4: Cross-selling – three 'Rules of 3s'

- **What?**
  - Product
  - Feature
  - Access
- **When?**
  - Upfront
  - Follow up (within 6 months)
  - At change points (product, customer)
- **How?**
  - Transitional product to term customers
  - Term products to transactional customers
  - 'Like to like': credit to credit customers, investments to deposit customers

Source: 3-i Inc.

Table 3.5: Why cross-selling? Why this way?

- **Builds loyalty – average retention rates**
  - 1 product: 90%
  - 2 products: 95%
  - 3 products: 98%
  - 4 products: 99%
- **Builds profit**
  - Cross-selling costs max. two-thirds of new sales and
  - Selling term product buys us time to cross-sell later
  - Selling transactional product ties customer to us and gives us information for better targeting later
  - Selling 'like to like' is easier than going against customers' behaviour

Source: 3-i Inc.

Table 3.6: Cross-selling – a simple template

Cross-sell the *products* below, to...

...customers holding...

	C/A (current Acct)	S/A (Savings Acct)	T/L (Term Loan)	L/C (Line of credit)	CC (credit card)	TD (Term Dep)
C/A		2			1	
S/A	1		2		3	2
T/L			1	2	2	3
L/C	1		2			
CC	3		2	1		
TD	3	2				1

... in the priority noted by '1', '2' or '3'

Source: 3-i Inc.

Now, on to service quality. This makes all the sense in the world – it makes money...

Table 3.7: Customer service quality

- **Why?**
  - It makes money
  - Customers want it
  - Hard to duplicate

- **Makes money - #1**
  - Western experience - $6,500 balances, +0.3 products
  - At 2% NIM and 100,000 customers this is $13 million / year

- **Makes money - #2**
  - Emerging market experience, 100,000 customers + 2,000/yr acquisitions (word of mouth) - 1,000/yr attention (1% decrease), + 10,000 products (+0.1/customer)
  - This equals 8,000 'new customer equivalent' (at 2 products / customer) and +$760,000/yr (at $95/yr/customer)
  - Cost of programme is $220,000 (training, tracking, other), hence 3.5 revenue / cost ratio and 3.5 month payback

Source: 3-i Inc.

However, we need to be careful that we understand very clearly what service quality actually means to our customers and what this requires from us as sales people. Service quality for our customers means efficient and consistent delivery of basic services at or above their expectations. It also means good advice and taking their problems away as our own if we cannot provide a solution on the spot. Finally, it means a certain way of relating to them that is friendly and respectful, always respecting the special relationship in which they are the boss.

Table 3.8: Service quality – for customers

• **Efficiency** – Everyday, basic services – Reliable, consistent – No frustration, no hassle, no problem – Quick but not hurried	• **Friendliness** – Calm, respectful – Honest, open, accessible – Competent, individual treatment – Overall character, tonality
• **Advice** – Address requests on the spot – Helpful, professional, competent – Offer (basic) solutions – Proactive	**NOTE:** – Easy banking is NOT private banking – Advice is NOT high end tax planning – Respect is NOT 'brotherly love' – CONSISTENCY is key

Source: 3-i Inc.

It follows that service quality is not a high-end 'blow your mind away' complex delivery. A number of studies have underlined this – and have been kept confidential by banks using their results, while watching others setting impossible service level goals for themselves at a high cost and missing the boat (customer needs) at the same time.

It is then fairly easy to translate well-researched customer needs into well-planned sales and service processes to deliver what is needed.

Table 3.9: Service quality – for the bank

• **I own the customer's problem** – No 'run around' for the customer
• **It is my job to know about baking, not his** – I should think ahead about his/her needs
• **I know that selling the right product is service** – Cross-selling is right!
• **I give my customers the option on how to contact/deal with us** – I do not monopolise the relationship (remember: service remotely...)
• **I know that everybody has customers, not only Sales** – All departments and functional areas must participate

Source: 3-i Inc.

There is a simple way of summarising what everyone in sales must do to deliver that great service. It is stated in Table 3.10 because I truly believe it is one of the most important things we must always keep in mind.

Table 3.10: Service quality – three things I must always do

- **"EVERY day, EVERY time, with no EXCEPTION, I will:**
  - Make banking with us easy – I will take the frustration out of your banking
  - Actively identify your financial needs and help you with professional advice
  - Treat you fairly, with respect and competence"
- **Doing the above will *inevitably* lead to success...**

Source: 3-i Inc.

'Doing it right is second nature'

There is a logical sequence to conducting a sales meeting with someone. In the best companies all sales people know this and follow the steps instinctively. It is worth remembering what these 'seven steps to sales success' are, as shown in Table 3.11.

Table 3.11: Seven steps to sales success

1. Greet warmly and openly
2. Address obvious needs and strong demands
3. Probe for hidden needs
4. Offer solutions to needs discovered
5. Confirm if solutions are acceptable or need to be changed
6. Close sale, agree steps
7. Follow up, analyse, learn

Source: 3-i Inc.

We will now leave this summary review and look at how one bank tested its way to success, by putting the right processes and structures in place. At the end of the case study we will once again review the lessons learned from doing it right, and reinforce just how easy it is to plan our way to inevitable sales success.

Case study 9: Pulling it all together

The bank used to illustrate this study is a large regional in Europe, with solid management and well-established sales structures / processes. It wanted to test the upside potential in its sales organisation, by implementing many of the best practices / processes reviewed in this chapter. It had the luxury of being present in several countries, with a multitude of branches, so selecting test locations could be done with great flexibility.

Indeed, in the first pilot test the location was selected by a competition among all branches in the selected test country. They had to bid for selection by making a case for why their branch would be a good location. This ensured strong commitment and support for the disciplines to be implemented as part of the pilot (an approach that is strongly recommended to any company thinking of doing a similar test). The test country itself was selected by head office based on commitment from local sales management.

The test was to utilise 'unused' capacity in the branches, to follow up central marketing activities and carry out targeted proactive sales activities to boost results. Because everyone believed the basics were in place, there were no new additional upfront training or process redesign steps taken. It was simply a question of 'using what we already have, more efficiently'.

Table 3.12: Case study 9 pilot test – outline

- **Set Up**
  - Built on training already done
  - Planned to use 'excess branch capacity'
  - Assumption: 'sales basics' in place

- **Key Elements**
  - Follow up on central marketing events
  - Corporate employee acquisition
  - Central DM follow-up
  - Proactive offer to walk-in prospects
  - Proactive, personal, cross-selling to customers

Source: 3-i Inc.

The results were puzzling. Year-on-year growth was much stronger in the test location than in the control one. But it was still well below objectives. In addition, most of the incremental results came not from branch staff, but from DSAs (commissioned mobile bankers) attached to the pilot location, who generated strong volume growth using the extra support.

Table 3.13: Case study 9 pilot test – results

Business growth (%)	2001 (Base)	2002 (Test)
Pilot location	+7	+21*
Control (Rest of Branches)	+10	+13

*Note:
1. 'All in' result would be +29%, without factoring out growth in DSA (Direct Sales Agent) number
2. Result would have been only +8% without any DSA support
3. Objective was +46%

Source: 3-i Inc.

On top of that, it quickly became obvious that extra sales efforts saved the day and results did not come about due to process improvements (as they were not upgraded anyway at the start). The best that could be said about the pilot was that it generated valuable information for a follow-up test.

Table 3.14: Case study 9 pilot test – successes and failures

- **Failure**
  – achieved less than 50% of target growth rate...
- **Success**
  – 300% growth acceleration vs 30% control...
- **Failure**
  – growth driven by effort of staff, not by process design...
- **Success**
  – valuable lessons for next phase

Source: 3-i Inc.

It became obvious that acquisition-focused channels (DSAs) need to be fully integrated into any test design. Similarly, when local sales management says "everything is OK, we have all the right processes in place", this should not be taken at face value. Processes need to be reviewed and upgraded as needed. A local opinion of what a good process is may not match global best expectations. Similarly, sales plans must be integrated into overall plans and objectives set appropriately, to avoid demotivating test participants.

In addition to integrating plans, support processes need to be reviewed for quality delivery. There was an obvious problem with the quality of call lists provided by the marketing department, yet this was not recognised until more than half way through the test. Individual performance tracking could not be implemented, yet this was not highlighted upfront. Finally, management's perspective that there was extra capacity in the system, waiting to be utilised was also overly optimistic.

Table 3.15: Case study 9 pilot test – evaluation

- ***Acquisition* focused channels / staff are essential (eg DSAs)**
  – DSAs drove 70+ % of growth
  – DSAs should be part of sales planning and linked to branches
- **Basic *sales* set up (process, etc.) should be addressed first**
  – Pre-training in proactive selling, incl. Management
  – Scripting, daily 'huddles', weekly sales meetings
- **Need *disciplined base* on which to build**
  – Objective was set too high
  – Individual objective setting and tracking are needed
- ***Marketing* quality and processes should also be reviewed**
  – Central mailing list not shared upfront
  – 20%+ error rate in list (hence only 3% call-to-meeting conversation vs. 10-15% benchmark)
- **Sales *effort* has saved the day – there *was* extra capacity in the system, even with existing set up**
  – Meeting-to-sales conversion 22% vs. 25-35% benchmark
  – 3x growth rate increase achieved even with missing elements and all effort as incremental
- **Capacity *planning* is key issue**
  – Admin work needs to be taken out before extra sales work is added in
  – IT support, process redesign, gatekeeper function, etc needed

Source: 3-i Inc.

Using this knowledge a new test site, in a different country, was selected and a number of changes made to the original test design.

Table 3.16: Case study 9 pilot test – lessons

- Focus on *sales process basics* to *build foundation* first
- Extend training to Sales Management
- *Integrate* DSAs and other channels into sales structure
- Individual level target setting and compensation needed
- Focus on *capacity planning* and key enablers for it

Source: 3-i Inc.

One interesting twist was to put local sales management through the same training as their sales staff had to do prior to start of the new pilot. This generated multiple benefits. Management understood what their staff must be capable of doing, so could follow results more closely and help out faster and better. At the same time, sales staff saw that their bosses went through the same training, so there was an immediate improvement in the level of trust with which they regarded their managers.

Table 3.17: Case study 9 second test – outline

• New test site, new country
• Use all learnings from Pilot 1
• No DSAs, higher branch traffic ('stress test')
• Central design and support, local ownership and implementation
• *Integrated approach* – **channels, training, capacity planning, marketing, sales processes and management**

Source: 3-i Inc.

An integrated sales approach was fully embraced and resulted in good alignment across all elements, processes, goals and departments. Sales capacity was taken seriously and used as a foundation on which to build activities.

Figure 3.1: Case study 9 second test – concept

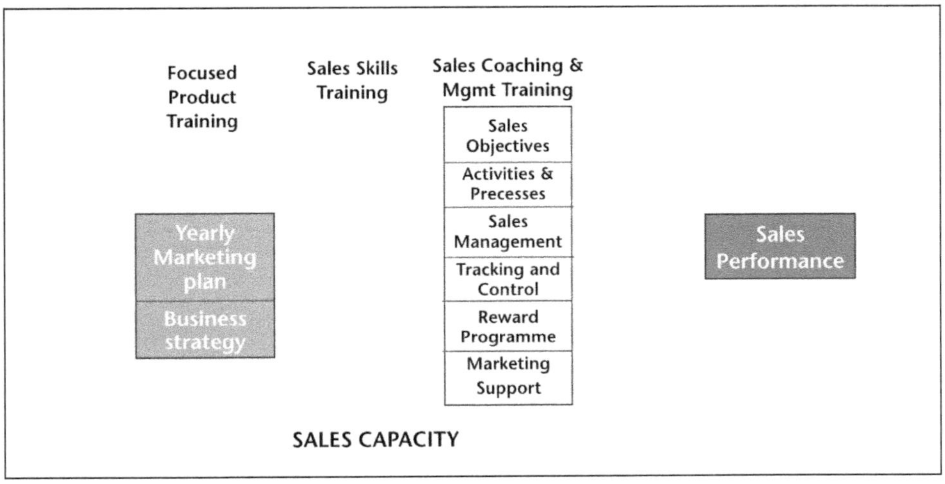

Source: 3-i Inc.

The existence of best sales practices was not taken for granted, but a rigorous sales process / sales management system was mandated to reflect global best benchmarks. This included individual tracking of leading indicators and efficiency ratios, meeting schedules for close tracking and well-integrated support from non-sales areas.

The support provided by non-sales areas (e.g. Marketing) was also quality controlled upfront, rather than accepting things as they had 'always used to be done'.

Table 3.18:Case study 9 second test – key components

- **Sales Objectives**
  – Number of selected (focus) products to be sold monthly, split by week and individual (no aggregated volume targets)
- **Sales Activities / Processes**
  – Introducing active part (outbound cross-sell calls) alongside standard passive one, structured approach and conversion stages, daily activity / opportunity planning per individual
- **Sales Management**
  – Daily, weekly, monthly sales meetings, formal coaching, on-going process planning and performance review (branch sales board), team work, sales effort enforcement
- **Tracking and Control**
  – Tracking the sales performance on a daily basis, per branch and front-line individual
- **Marketing Support**
  – Cross-sell prospect list selection with opportunity rating
- **Reward Scheme**
  – Simple prize based scheme (e.g. dinners)

Source: 3-i Inc.

At the same time, all efforts were made to keep things simple. For example, research among employees showed that complicated reward systems would not add much to efficiencies, so the reward structure was kept very simple and easy to understand.

Tables 3.19 and 3.20 summarise some of the key enablers put in place and the sales meeting / sales monitoring structure implemented.

Table 3.19: Case study 9 second test – key enablers

- **Branch Sales Capacity**
  – Branch sales capacity measured before start and used for objective set-up and daily activity planning (incl. assessment of the spare capacity routinely utilised)
- **Sales Management and Product Training**
  – Sales process training utilising standardisation regional process
  – Sales coaching & management training, standard regional approach
  – Phone conversation (outbound) and scripting
  – Focus product re-training (sales process / benefit oriented)
- **Branch Site**
  – Model branch in good location but competitive city area
  – 7,000 customers with balanced portfolio

Source: 3-i Inc.

Table 3.20: Case study 9 second test – sales meetings structure

Daily

- 5-10 minute daily 'warm-up' covering a short recap of the last day's results and focusing the team for new day's objectives / priorities

Weekly

- Results recap and new week's planning and objectives highlight
- Address successes and identify improvement areas
- Recognise best performer(s)
- Ensure brief sharing of the team learnings
- Identify support required / expected

Monthly

- Review monthly sales performance and activities per branch and individual
- Celebrate successes and recognise the best performer(s)
- Gather staff feedback, share and review learnings
- Address and plan for improvement areas
- Plan for the next month and highlight the objectives

Source: 3-i Inc.

Actual sales activity tracking relied on monitoring leading indicators (and, hence, conversion efficiencies) as well as actual results. This gave management a tool to continuously improve things and also provided the executive with an ongoing update on actual results – securing its continued support.

Table 3.21: Case study 9 second test – sales planning

ACTIVE GROUP SALES BOARD											
December 2003		Calls	Contacts	Meetings	Sales						
					Current Account	D/D	Deposits	Personal loans	Mortgage	Credit Cards	Others
	8										
	9										
	10										
	11										
	12										
Week 1	Actual										
	Objective										
	15										
	16										
	17										
	18										
	19										
Week 2	Actual										
	Objective										
	22										
	23										
	24										
Week 3	Actual										
	Objective										
	29										
	30										
	31										
Week 4	Actual										
	Objective										
Month	Actual										
	Objective										

Source: 3-i Inc.

Both efficiency ratios and actual results showed very positive trends.

Table 3.22: Case study 9 second test – efficiency ratios

	Dec	Jan			Feb		
Base	**Salary**	**Salary**	**CC pre-approved**	**Non-active Current Accounts**	**Non-active Current Accounts**	**External**	**Loans**
Product to be sold	O/D	Deposits	Credit Card	Various	Various	Credit Card	Credit Card
Callable to initial list	31%	60%	94%	84%	100%	100%	95%
Contacts to initial list	18%	34%	40%	38%	52%	75%	66%
Contacts to callable list	59%	56%	43%	45%	52%	75%	70%
Meetings planned to initial list	9%	31%	29%	25%	34%	65%	38%
Meetings planned to callable list	28%	52%	31%	38%	34%	65%	40%
Meetings planned to contacts	47%	91%	72%	65%	66%	87%	57%
Meetings held to initial list	3%	28%	23%	15%	23%	23%	15%
Meetings held to callable list	9%	44%	24%	18%	23%	23%	16%
Meetings held to contacts	15%	77%	56%	40%	45%	30%	23%
Meetings held to planned	32%	84%	78%	61%	69%	35%	41%
Products sold to initial list	1%	16%	15%	13%	22%	43%	6%
Products sold to callable list	4%	26%	16%	16%	22%	43%	6%
Products sold to contacts	8%	46%	38%	35%	42%	57%	9%
Products sold to meetings planned	16%	50%	52%	54%	84%	65%	16%
Products sold to meetings held	50%	59%	67%	88%	93%	189%	38%

Source: 3-i Inc.

For example, term deposit results clearly show when focused activities started and new practices were put in place. This was true for both overall results and for results per front-office officer (proactive sales person in the branch). The same held true for other product areas as well, such as personal loans and credit cards.

The best news, however, was that deposit sales did not suffer when the focus shifted to another product area. This gave sales management the idea to further refine the processes and take into account the 'residual effect' of becoming proficient in one area as something they can count on in the future, even if focus shifts. We'll come back to this later.

Figure 3.2: Case study 9 second test – term deposit results 1

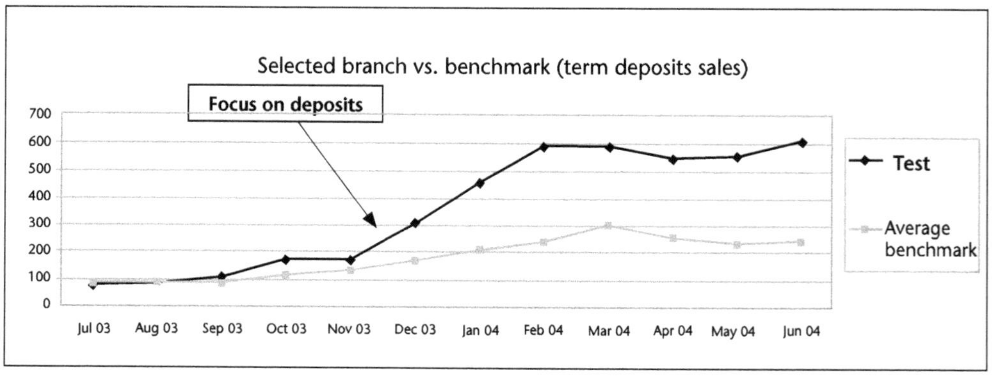

Source: 3-i Inc.

Figure 3.3: Case study 9 second test – term deposit results 2

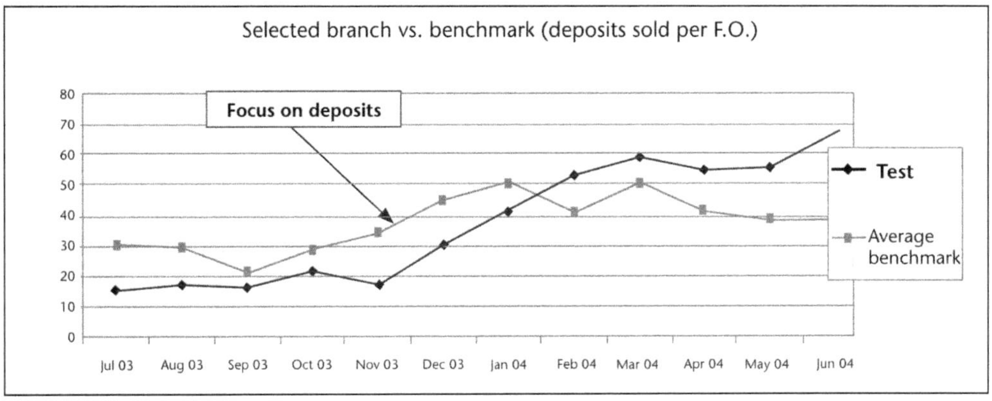

Source: 3-i Inc.

Figure 3.4: Case study 9 second test – loan results 1

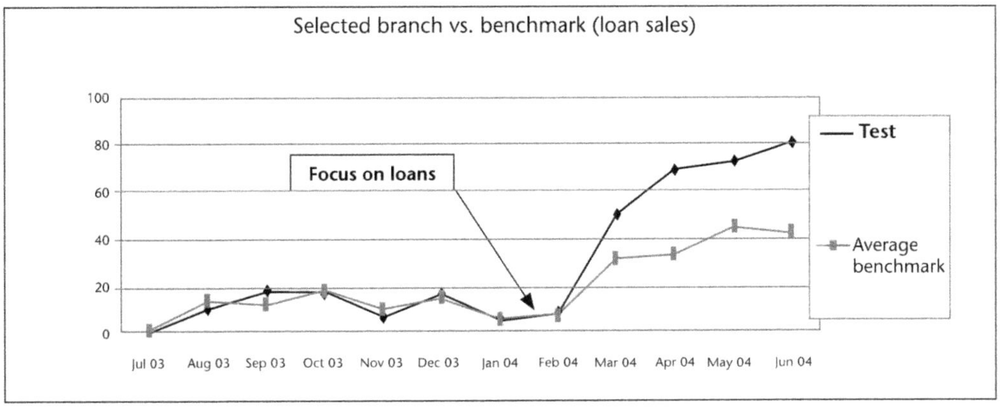

Source: 3-i Inc.

Figure 3.5: Case study 9 second test – loan results 2

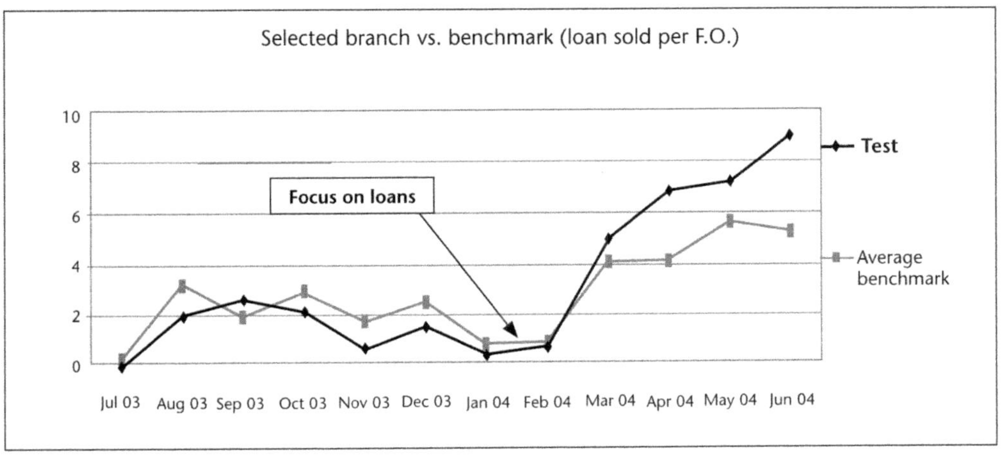

Source: 3-i Inc.

However, a word of caution: while the pilot study focused on specific products at a time, the bank made sure there was no compromise on the 'needs-based selling' approach. So a product push did not mean selling something at all costs. It simply meant taking advantage of market seasonalities and offering the best solutions to existing needs. This is a key item that should be remembered by all sales and marketing people wishing to apply lessons from this case study.

Figure 3.6: Case study 9 second test – credit card results 1

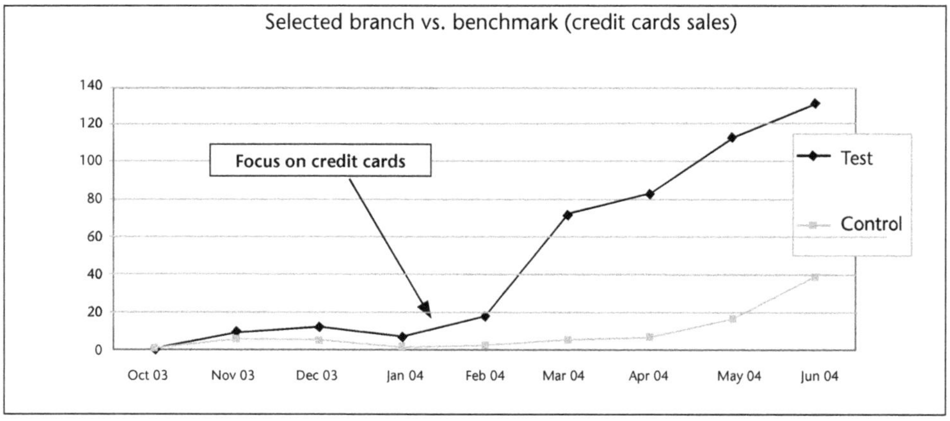

Source: 3-i Inc.

Figure 3.7: Case study 9 second test – credit card results 2

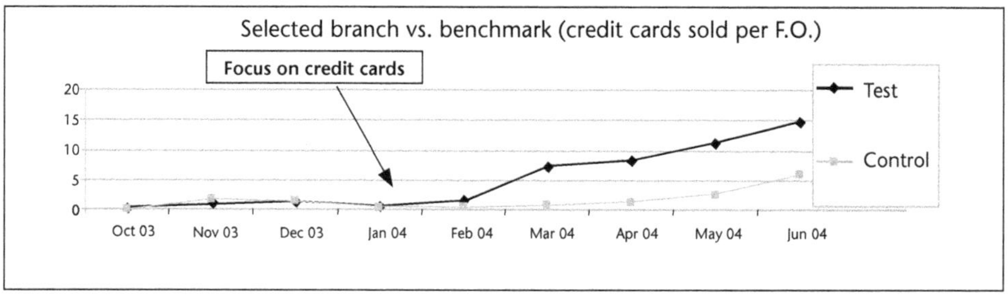

Source: 3-i Inc.

Interestingly, both customers and sales staff seemed to appreciate the new approach. This was a surprise – management initially thought the opposite would happen.

First, it was thought that sales staff would resent the extra pressure put on them by daily monitoring of activities. Instead, sales people appreciated the structured approach that inevitably led them to success. They appreciated even more the fact that they therefore ensured their bonuses would be earned! This led to half the branch managers lobbying management to expand the pilot as soon as possible, or at least to include them in it. (Management listened: the time of the pilot was cut in half and the programme rolled out nationally without any further regional tests – with good results ...)

Second, management was afraid that customers and prospects would resent the heavy sales push, as a 'shoving something down their throat' approach. Instead, consumers liked this new attention to their needs and the obvious effort sales staff put into understanding these needs and offering solutions. Customer satisfaction scores (already tracked quarterly at branch level) went up significantly and beat control results.

Figure 3.8: Case study 9 second test – service quality results

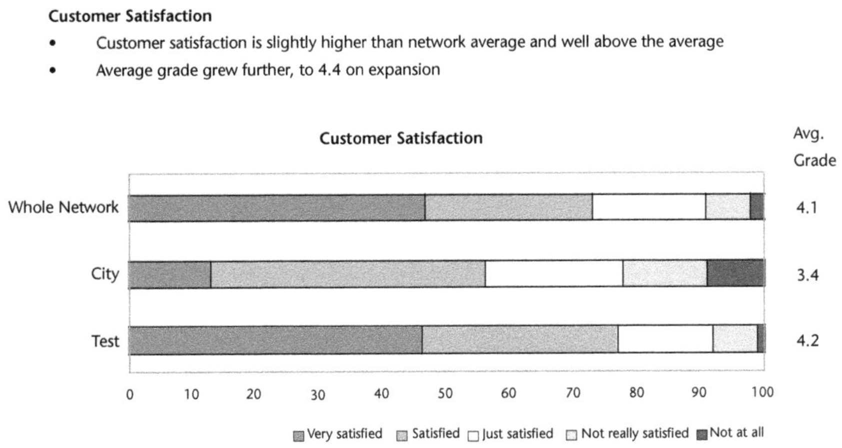

Source: 3-i Inc.

As mentioned before, the pilot was accelerated based on the excellent results seen and management decided to roll out nationally. While this may have been a risky decision, it was mitigated by several items.

Table 3.23: Case study 9 – roll-out

- Key objective – quickly roll-out basis of the sales performance culture into most important branch outlets and regions and increase average sales

↓

- Narrow some of the sales set-up components to allow quick and practical application across a number of branches of varying business environment
  – Product Focus – credit card (consumer loan top-up)
  – Branch Activity Focus – warm sales leads and sales meetings

↓

- Call centre to make contacts based on pre-selected lists and arrange meetings at branches (centrally available individual calendars, standard mail messages)
- Dedicated branch staff to be available for 'remote' arrangements

Source: 3-i Inc.

There was a gradual roll-out schedule put in place, including the better-prepared units first. The processes were also refined further, to essentially 'guarantee' success.

And success was indeed achieved. Efficiency ratios improved further as all previous lessons were incorporated.

Table 3.24: Case study 9 roll-out – efficiencies

4 May –19 Aug	Actual	Objective
Calling lists	4,138	4,138
Wrong numbers	172	207
	4%	5%
Unreachable	468	414
	11%	10%
People reached	3,498	3,517
	85%	85%
Meetings	1,185	1,103
from people reached	34%	31%
		381
Applications	920	11%
from people reached	26%	35%
from meetings	78%	322
		85%
Credit Cards	855	8%
from applications	93%	9%
from total calling list	21%	
from people reached	24%	
	No	**% applications**
*pending	5	1%
approved	855	93%
rejected	50	5%
sent back	10	1%

Source: 3-i Inc.

Sales results followed…

Figure 3.9: Case study 9 roll-out – credit card results 1

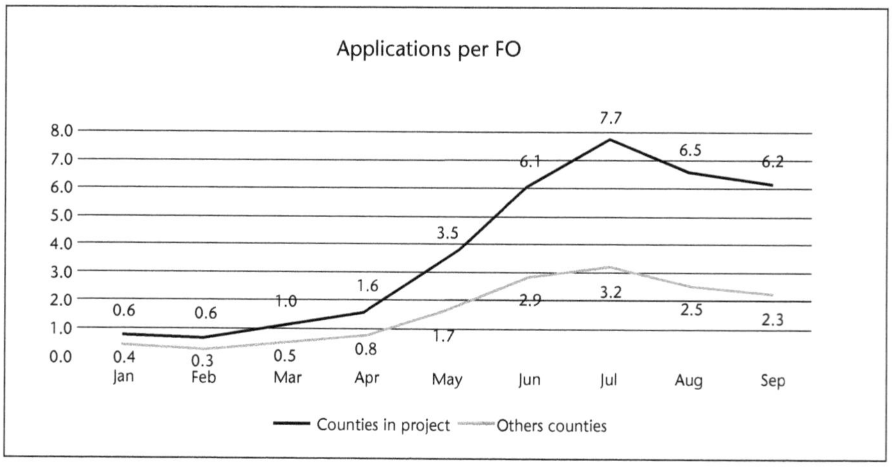

Source: 3-i Inc.

Figure 3.10: Case study 9 roll-out – credit card results 2

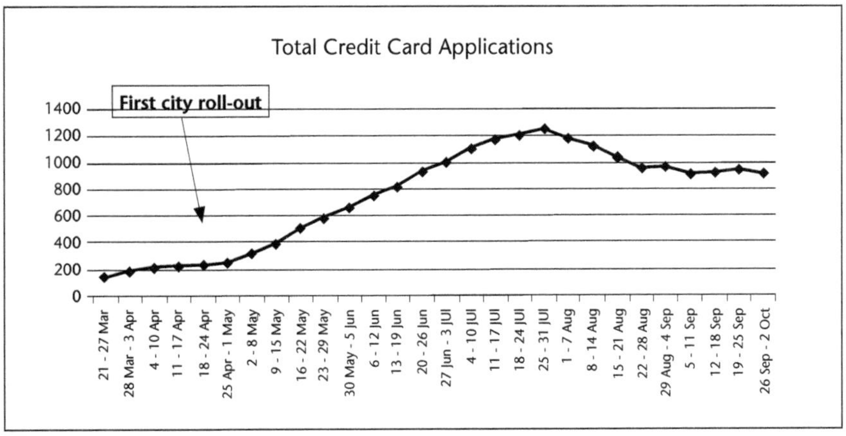

Source: 3-i Inc.

As mentioned before, management understood how it could rely on 'residual effects' and make plans accordingly. Here is one example how they put this into action. Obviously, cross-selling to existing customers is easier than cold calling new prospects. So it would make sense to get sales staff used to the fine art of phone selling by practicing first on 'easy targets' (branch customers) then hope that the learning they got from this exercise (that 'residual effect') would carry over into the more difficult area of cold calling. And indeed, this is exactly what happened.

Figure 3.11: Case study 9 roll-out – cross-sell vs. prospecting

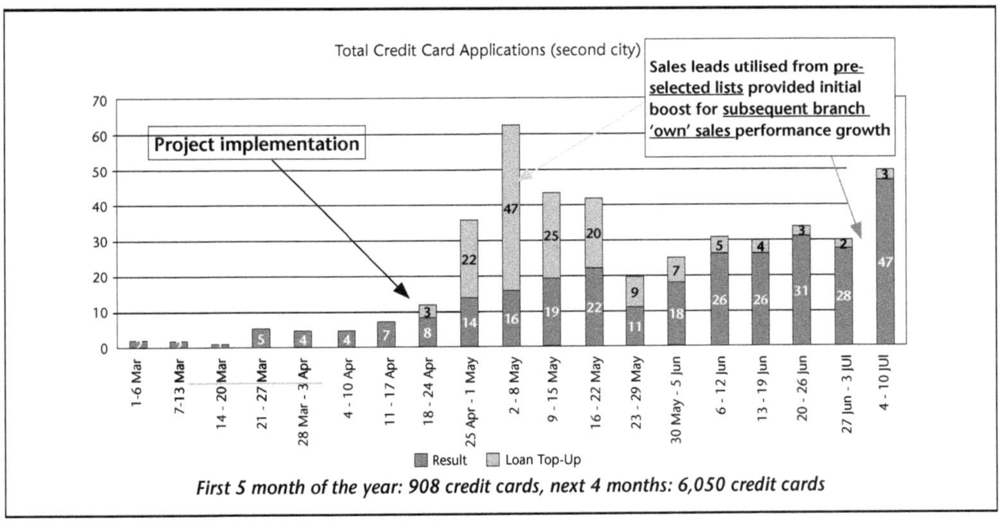

Source: 3-i Inc.

Figure 3.11 shows how starting with cross-selling improved sales results to existing clients, then how (after this pool of opportunity was used up) this carried over into getting prospect targets – a much more difficult job. An example of learning to walk before you can run, if ever there was one.

To recap, Table 3.25 summarises the lessons learned from this case study.

Table 3.25: Case study 9 – lessons

- **Yes, you can boost your branch sales (beyond expectations... regardless of environment...)**
- **Build the foundation first**
  – fit with sales / marketing plans
  – capacity planning
  – marketing support
- **Integrate all elements**
  – channels
  – training
  – sales management
  – sales processes
- **Performance tracking should be:**
  – individual
  – based on leading indicators and
  – conversion efficiencies
- **Customers appreciate proactive sales approach – your service quality measures should improve**
- **Sales staff are motivated by success – your employee satisfaction survey results should also improve**
- **If you have a Centre of Excellence, use it to design and set up the pilot, then to template and transfer learnings**

Source: 3-i Inc.

I hope the details of these tests and the factual information (ratios, etc.) will give the reader a ground-level understanding of how to design such tests and how to set objectives for them. It may be useful to quickly recap some of the best sales practices that drove the success just reviewed.

Table 3.26: Best sales practices summary

- **Selling may be an art, but *the sales process must be a disciplined science***
- **Everybody and *every department should sell***
- **Branches need to focus on *cross selling and service quality* to build relationships**
- **You can *plan your way to success* using leading indicators and efficiency ratios**
- **All sales-related steps must be *integrated* to deliver results**
- **Remember**
  – 'Rule of 3s' for Cross-selling
  – 'Seven Steps' to Sales Success'
  – The three 'Musts' to Deliver Service Quality
- **Cross-sell term products to translated customers and vice versa**
- **Cross-sell 'like to like'**
- **Seven Steps to Sales Success**
  – <u>Greet</u> warmly and openly
  – <u>Address</u> obvious needs and strong demands
  – <u>Probe</u> for hidden needs
  – <u>Offer</u> solutions to needs discovered
  – <u>Confirm</u> if solutions are acceptable or need to be changed
  – <u>Close</u> sale, agree next steps
  – <u>Follow up</u>, analyse, learn
- **The three 'Musts' for service quality**
  'EVERY day, EVERY time, with NO Exception, I will:
  – Make banking with us easy – I will take the frustration out of your banking
  – Actively identify your financial needs and help you with professional advice
  – Treat you fairly, with respect and competence'
- **Finally...**
  – Results are *inevitable* if you 'plan your way to success'
  – You can do it!

Source: 3-i Inc.

Chapter 4
Promoting change – implementation guide for best practices

Introduction

Change is difficult. Change is resisted by employees. Change is resisted by management. Yet change is an absolute must.

The best sales practices reviewed so far represent more or less a change for most banks.

How to sell the change? Just as importantly: What is involved in the change, how long does it take, what resources are needed, how to monitor results? Once someone has bought into the concepts presented here, these questions become the most important ones to answer. This chapter is to help the reader develop the answers and plan implementation.

Let us consider a hypothetical scenario: if the reader was a consultant who has a proposal and needs to sell it to a bank, he would have to clearly articulate all the answers. He would also have to discuss the background to the proposal, and how and why it fits into the bank's plans.

Doing the same from the inside is not that different. After all, we are all 'consultants' in our daily jobs, selling our ideas to management and justifying our salaries.

So what better way to illustrate what is involved in selling, planning and executing the implementation of best sales practice than using a scenario where the reader (the 'consultant') has to present his plans to the buyer – the bank? What follows is just such an exercise.

To keep things simple, I have used my own name and company (3-i Inc.) as the ones making the pitch. I have called the bank simply 'the Bank'. I have assumed it is a leading bank in a mid-sized emerging market, with its own share of problems in terms of lack of clean customer data, etc, for the sake of being more realistic. It is owned by a parent company in a developed market.

For those unfamiliar with 'consultant speak', Phase 0 refers to a preliminary assessment of the situation, enabling a proposal to be made. Phase 1 usually refers to the first deliverable, such as a test. Phase 2 is the follow-up deliverable, for example a national roll-out. Enjoy the change of pace and style!

The proposal

This proposal is made for the Bank (the Client) by 3-i Inc. (the Supplier), whose president / CEO is Sandy Vaci (the Consultant).

Content

- Background / overview – findings of Phase 0;
- Objectives / deliverables – benefits of Phase 1;
- Measuring success – decision framework;
- Delivery options – timing, cost, methodology;

- Roles / responsibilities – supplier and client;
- Terms and conditions – payments, confidentiality.

At the end of this proposal there will be a detailed overview of timing, resources needed, specific next steps and their deliverables to help the Bank decide about moving forward or not – based on a full understanding of all requirements. This will include:

- Project phases and options;
- The Bank's resource requirements;
- Phase 1 building blocks;
- Phase 1 and 2 options – details.

Background / overview – findings of Phase 0 (already completed)

The Bank is one of the two leading banks in its market. It has recently implemented a branch efficiency project (BEP) which clearly defined staff roles in branches and reduced resource requirements to do business. There is an opportunity to build on results of the BEP by implementing world class sales processes and sales management practices on this new infrastructure, coupled with 'best in class' sales, database and marketing support programmes. Both management and staff seem to support this approach. Sandy Vaci has been asked to review the situation and submit a proposal on how this could be done.

Primary focus of the proposed activities should be to boost retail lending results, to gain significant net interest margin (NIM) improvements for the retail banking unit – in line with the Bank's stated objectives for the next financial year. The selected approach should therefore enable the organisation to cross-sell / up-sell personal loans to its existing customer base in the most efficient manner. The practices implemented should of course be usable to boost sales of other offers. Focus should be kept on personal bankers and BDRs (business development representatives) in the branches, with support from alternative channels (such as the customer care centre) and central units (such as marketing) as needed to achieve results. Credit card and SME sales forces, as well as full alternative delivery channel integration and other components should be addressed later, after the success of a mostly retail lending-focused, branch-based initiative.

Traditional global best practices to boost cross-sell rely on reliable database information about existing customers. This is not possible at the Bank because only 20% or less of existing customer records can be used to drive activities. While data cleansing has started, it is not expected to deliver results in time to support efficient cross-selling (only 'A' customer records will be 'clean' and only by September 2006, which is near the expected end date of the sales boost pilot). Current data input is also inadequate, with only 50% of records booked being 'clean'. Finally, the Bank's CRM set-up lacks front-end sales force automation / lead management and marketing database analytical capabilities. Complicating matters is the high transactional workload evident at all branches and high level of manual service to provide outstanding customer experience.

Because of the above, the best approach would rely strongly on turning the existing heavy branch traffic to the Bank's advantage for cross-selling, but supported by customer information-driven activities as much as possible. An integrated three-pronged approach should be used:

1. Target customers coming into the branches directly with specific sales offers, to start a significant sales push even with a lot of customer information still missing;
2. Implement marketing activities to gather missing customer information and carry on with cleansing the information already in the system – concurrently with point 1 above;
3. Incremental sales activities using the (limited) customer information available today, utilising alternative channels to support branch efforts as much as possible.

The above approach should be based on the most efficient global best practices sales processes and sales management practices – in a way which allows for immediate results while keeping flexibility for further improvement later. The approach should be tested in four branches of various sizes and locations and allow for shifting to heavier reliance on central database support as reliable customer information becomes more available. To help this, and as mentioned above, gathering and cleansing customer information should be addressed at the same time.

Finally, local Bank resources should be used as much as possible to ensure lessons learned from the pilot are retained within the Bank for sustainable, long-term benefits. This should also keep consulting fees and costs to a minimum – both during the pilot phase and for an eventual national roll-out.

Objectives / deliverables – benefits of Phase 1

At the end of the 26-week / six-month Phase 1 the Bank should have:

- Four branches in full test mode, using global best practice sales processes and sales management set-up to generate significant cross-sell / up-sell improvements on personal loans;
- The above sales processes and sales management practices documented and templated for national roll-out – with non-exclusive but time unlimited right of ownership of all methods and materials developed for, and accepted by, the Bank (e.g. individual objective setting and activity planning, integrated crosssell processes, sales coaching and performance tracking, etc.);
- All processes and methodologies designed for existing Bank / local market realities but structured in a flexible way to allow evolution later on with minimal extra work;
- The required additional training modules and pilot branch personnel trained in their use to deliver results (e.g. prospecting, cross-selling, scripting, objection handling, competitive positioning);

- An integrated support system design (marketing, IT, operations, credit, alternative channels) to the extent that they are needed to make the pilot a success;
- Roll-out plan outline with timing, resources, activities, deliverables;
- Fully trained head office resources to implement roll-out on a national basis with minimal consulting support required, and to modify the approach ongoing as needed in response to changing conditions;
- Organisational acceptance of the new sales approach, as measured by feedback from sales staff and management and by solicited comments from other functional areas.

The overall objective is to enable the Bank's retail banking division to implement the most efficient ways to generate profits on a sustainable basis, as compared to global best practices, based on market and Bank realities. Phase 1 therefore should:

- Put the infrastructure in place for this;
- Test it for best implementation locally; and
- Train local resources to quickly and successfully expand it.

Measuring success – decision framework

Success of the project can be measured at five different levels:

A Project execution;

B Infrastructure implementation;

C Business results;

D Payback and project efficiency;

E Residual benefits.

A) Project execution

- Progress and critical items reviewed at monthly meetings with executive management;
- Ongoing feedback solicited and documented;
- Regular (monthly) written project updates to document progress and highlight issues.

B) Infrastructure implementation

Evaluate whether the promised sales set-up is complete and is functioning to expectations. This is the area covered in 'Objectives / deliverables' above. In effect, this measures all the different dimensions of success in providing the tools to the Bank's staff to drive results – which are the main objectives of Phase 1. It should tell us if the implemented processes and management practices should work efficiently in the given local environment, and whether we should expect the organisation to be able to deliver improved results based on the new methods put in place.

C) Business results

Measuring business results can be done in three different ways:

1. Evaluating early trends in leading indicators, such as efficiency of booking sales meetings;
2. Measuring initial results and projecting them to estimate ultimate success rate;
3. Reading ongoing results to ensure confirmed, sustainable success has been achieved.

1) Expected success – early trends

Early trends can be read relatively soon – within two to three weeks of pilot start-up. Key success factors to look at include efficiency ratios of early leading indicators, such as ratio of calls to meetings booked. As long as infrastructure implementation (see above) was done successfully, these early indicators could be projected out based on experience in other markets and companies to indicate expected success based on the new setup implemented.

2) Projected success – initial results

Reading initial results depends on how far in advance sales meetings need to be booked and how fast the Bank can through-process loan applications. If, for example, it takes four weeks from the initial call to have the sales meeting, close the sale and disburse the loan, then a six-week minimum monitoring period is needed to read initial results – to allow for at least two weeks of data to be generated. The advantage of this approach is that success can be projected using 'own information', without relying on external data. The disadvantage is the additional time needed compared with reading early trends.

3) Confirmed success – ongoing results

Measuring ongoing results is needed to confirm sustainable improvements without doubt. Ongoing results take longer to read. They include, for example, customer satisfaction survey results and the confirmed ability of the organisation to sustain sales momentum without adding extra resources. Based on timing of customer service quality surveys and business planning cycles, this can take several months after early indicators have already confirmed the success of a new sales programme.

D) Payback and project efficiency

Payback for the project can be derived by calculating the incremental volumes (such as personal loan balances) that need to be generated behind improved sales efficiencies to pay for total project costs. These required improvements should then be compared with gains experienced behind similar initiatives elsewhere to judge the reasonableness of payback expectations.

For personal loans, for example, NIMs assigned to the incremental volume should reflect the incremental margin to be made by placing funds as retail loans versus wholesale lending. Shifts in sales activities from reactive to proactive, and their resultant volume lift, also need to be factored in. Project costs should reflect consulting fees and other out-of-pocket expenses, plus dedicated full-time equivalent (FTE) costs at the Bank.

3-i Inc. has done preliminary payback calculations using 'best assumptions' and confirmed the project to be worthwhile before submitting this proposal. However, this exercise needs to be undertaken by the Client, using internal information, to have real validity. Therefore, 3-i Inc.'s findings are omitted here. However, help and support is available from 3-i Inc. as needed by the Bank in the course of these calculations.

Cost efficiency of the project (as executed by 3-i Inc.) could be assessed by comparing competing bids for the same scope and expected outcome. 3-i Inc. did a competitive cost comparison, recalculating its fees using standard charge rates by established consultancies. This showed a substantial cost advantage for 3-i Inc.'s proposal as it is submitted here. The Bank is welcome to verify these findings.

Please note, however, that verification needs to be done on a 'pure' basis, with 'fresh' bidding. Absolutely no part of this proposal may be shared with any other firm or individual in the course of doing so. The amount and level of information presented here reflect significant effort already invested by 3-i Inc. Sharing it with competitive firms or anyone else may cause significant, irreparable and incalculable, damage to 3-i Inc. and must therefore be prevented.

E) Residual benefits

These benefits would most likely accrue at the 'owner' (Bank parent) level. They relate to having a 'standard of excellence'" in the Bank, in terms of global best sales practices, after successful completion of the 'sales boost' roll-out. This means that the Bank could be used as a source of best practices and proven business methods in any expansion into other markets that either the Bank or the Bank parent may undertake in the future.

For example, when setting up a business or acquiring control in another market the knowledge of the Bank could readily be transferred and its management talent utilised to ensure rapid improvements, or a speedy start-up, with guaranteed results. Realising these benefits would require additional market entries and would depend on many unforeseen factors. Because of this, these benefits cannot easily be quantified.

It is recommended that 'D' level calculations form the basis for the decision of whether or not to engage in the project with 3-i Inc. Level 'E' benefits are a 'nice to have' but should not be used to drive an engagement decision because they are too hard to quantify. (However, they may form the basis for a request of project cost sharing at the Bank parent level.)

'A', 'B' and 'C-1' level results together should be used to track success and decide about expansion of Phase 1.

Phase 1A project timing (see below) should allow management to make an expansion decision six months after start of the pilot based on the above.

There is reasonable evidence from previous experience to support the above recommendation on expansion decision-making. Similar set-ups in emerging market environments have shown substantial success in sales efficiencies (twoto fivefold efficiency gains), organisational acceptance (full buy-in at the branch manager level) and customer acceptance (between no-decline to significant-gains in customer satisfaction scores). See the Attachments at the end of this chapter for background on past results achieved with similar initiatives.

However, it is entirely the Bank management's decision as to how aggressively they wish to move forward and what level of reassurance they need before deciding on expansion. Achieving the above quoted-results at the Bank cannot be guaranteed. Results at the end will depend on the ability of the local organisation to execute, ongoing, the processes and practices implemented. Success will also depend on local bank management decisions and support, and may be influenced by unforeseen market activities. However, the know-how imparted, effort planned and approach to be used will be the same as those that generated the above-mentioned results in similar emerging market settings.

Delivery options – timing, cost, methodology

Phase 1A

The 'Objectives / deliverables' section details deliverables and benefits for Phase 1, Option A. This option (Phase 1A) is the recommended way of starting the project. It would focus on personal bankers and BDRs, set up a pilot in four branches, address the issues of lack of customer information, new marketing / sales support approach and alternative channel integration to the extent that they are needed to deliver on the objectives stated in the Objectives / deliverables section. It would allow for a fast start-up and limit costs while maintaining later flexibility. Note that a full description of different phasing options is provided in the case study at the end of this chapter.

Although primary product focus would be on personal loans, the processes and management practices developed could equally be used to support other product sales initiatives. The pilot will need to carefully balance two key components:

1. Relationship banking focus – ensure customers are offered the right solutions to their individual circumstances;
2. Sales capacity allocation – allocate time available for proactive selling to the highest priority single product to avoid confusion and generate best results.

Timing

- Phase 1A can be started three weeks after agreement is reached between the Client and the Supplier, assuming the Bank provides the legal / regulatory and logistical support to start the engagement. Details of the latter are outlined further on, under 'Responsibilities of Client'.
- This Phase is targeted to take six months and should not exceed eight months, allowing for unforeseen issues. This estimate is based on the assumption that the support requirements as outlined in Attachment 2 are met by the Client and management / executive decisions regarding direction and alternatives are provided within three working days of issues presented.

Cost

- Consulting fees of C$[xxx], payable net to 3-i Inc. / Sandy Vaci. This fee represents 1.25 FTE consulting engagement for six months (at a 30% 'longterm engagement discount' versus standard daily rates). This fee is net of applicable local taxes and levies. Applicable Canadian taxes and levies are the responsibility of 3-i Inc. and should be considered as included in the above.
- Additional out-of-pocket expense reimbursements, provisions of safe and adequate local accommodation, transportation and travel expenses from/ to [the Bank's offices in yyy] for the Consultants. Given that most of the work (75%+) should be carried out locally, and given the required level of consulting support, the following may be assumed for planning purposes:
  - Six to eight months (joint) accommodation for one to two persons in [yyy];
  - Six to nine round-trip tickets from Toronto to [yyy];
  - Two round-trip tickets from continental Europe to [yyy].

Methodology

The methodology uses a six-part 'building block' approach as described in detail in the case study.

Other Phase 1 alternatives and follow-up Phase 2 options are covered in the following paragraphs. While this proposal recommends starting with Phase 1A, the other alternatives are offered for consideration at the sole discretion of the Client.

Phase 1B

This approach would build on Phase 1A and add a full CRM / marketing programme review. It would require an additional 0.25 FTE consulting support and cost a corresponding C$[xxx] more. The total cost therefore would be C$[xxx] plus expenses. This option can be accommodated with currently available consulting resources and be executed during the same six-month time frame as Option 1A, with additional consulting support. It is recommended, however, that the lower cost Option 1A be pursued and CRM and marketing issues be addressed only to the extent that they need to be for the success of the initial sales pilot.

Phases 1C and 1D

Option 1C would add customer base and product design / processing reviews to Option 1B. The benefits of this would be to address the high percentage of nonprofitable customers and identify ways of improving profitability by changing product definitions and processing / customer service standards.

Option 1D would include full alternative (remote, electronic) delivery channel reviews and process redesigns to Option 1C. Benefits would be to implement a global 'best in class' integrated channel strategy for most efficient customer acquisition, relationship deepening, retention and servicing. This would tie back to the best practice sales processes and sales management principles implemented for branches as part of Option 1A.

Both Options 1C and 1D may require consulting resources (minimum additional 0.5 FTE and 0.75 FTE, respectively) that cannot currently be guaranteed by 3-i Inc. For this reason, and to allow the Bank to see the benefits of the Supplier's help, it is recommended that these options be considered only at a later stage.

Phase 2A

Phase 2A refers to the speedy national roll-out ('Big Bang' approach) of the sales boost pilot, based on favourable early results, using mostly internal resources trained by the Consultant(s) during Phase 1. This Option should be doable in two– to six months and with minimal consulting support, limiting consulting fees to the C$[xxx–xxx] range.

The start of this phase would depend on the Bank management's decision on the level of success measurement from Phase 1. If, as recommended, management decides based on level A, B and C-1 measures, Phase 2 could start six months after the start of Phase 1 (and no longer than eight months after Phase 1 starts, allowing for unforeseen circumstances).

The length of this phase would depend primarily on resources available to do all the staff training that may be required and the organisation's ability to implement change. The Bank's recent BEP implementation experience suggests the latter should not pose a bottleneck.

Ideally, the roll-out could be done on a differentiated basis across all branches. Different branches may need different primary product focus, based on type of prospects in the trade area, existing customer base and level of product penetration within the latter. We need to be cautious, however: being able to do a 'differentiated' roll-out would require a quantity and quality of information very rarely available in emerging markets. It cannot be assumed that the Bank's current market would be different.

Phase 2B

Phase 2B would add SME and credit card sales focus to the national roll-out. This could be done either by duplicating the process / management set-up implemented for personal loans for the roll-out, or by starting a new pilot phase for SME and/ or credit cards at the same time as the original Phase 1 is being expanded. The preliminary time estimate for this phase is no more than six months, assuming the 'duplicate' approach. Consulting fees would vary based on internal knowledge and resources available and are expected to be between C$[xxx] and C$[xxx].

Roles / responsibilities – supplier and client

Responsibilities of consultant / supplier

- Know-how transfer and project leadership;
- On-site support as required – expected to be 75% of time or greater;
- Ensure adequate and qualified consulting support is available from both Sandy Vaci and others as it may be needed (see Attachment 1 to the case study, on potential additional consulting resources);
- Timely updates to management (monthly reports and update meetings) reviewing progress and flagging potential issues;
- Ensure local head office staff participating in project are trained in the sales process and sales management set-up methodology, to allow national roll-out using mostly local resources;
- Full documentation of processes, methods;
- Competent, co-operative, highest quality 'best effort' approach to project and solving issues;
- Flexibility in responding to unforeseen changes or new developments that may impact the project;
- Non-additional expenses of Consultant(s), such as meals and general living costs, not including accommodation and travel-related costs;
- Applicable Canadian taxes and regulatory compliance;
- Compliance with the Terms and Conditions as outlined in the next section.

Responsibilities of client

- Local regulatory compliance and logistics as needed: local work and other permit as required, taxes, fees, social security contributions, compliance with local regulations for such a project;
- Safe, adequate accommodation and travel expenses as outlined under 'Delivery Options';
- Coverage for local emergencies for Consultants – medical and other if needed;
- Local office and admin support for on-site work: space, equipment, logistical support;
- Resources as outlined in the case study;
- Timely business decisions and directions as they relate to the project: decisions in no more than three working days, feedback in no more than two working days, senior management availability for monthly review meetings;

- Informing the Supplier / Consultant immediately if there are unforeseen changes or developments that impact the project;
- All decisions affecting the Bank's business and their impact / results;
- Compliance with the Terms and Conditions as outlined below.

Terms and conditions

Payments

(These details are not relevant to this proposal.)

Confidentiality

- Any proprietary or confidential information learned about each other's businesses, processes, methods, plans will be kept confidential by both the Supplier and the Client. Information within each organisation will be distributed on a need-to-know basis;
- This confidentiality agreement will apply to employees leaving the Client, additional consulting resources brought in by the Supplier and any new business entity on either side that continues with a substantial part of either the Client's or the Supplier's activities;
- The Supplier retains intellectual property rights to all its methods, processes and approaches shared with or implemented at the Client. However, the Supplier gives the Client an irrevocable, royalty-free, time-unlimited, nonexclusive licence to use any and all such property as long as all the Terms and Conditions outlined in this section are met by the Client;
- Ideas and approaches rejected by the Client will remain the sole property of the Supplier. Note, therefore, if this proposal is not accepted no part of it may be used in any way by the Client and all copies of it must be returned to the Supplier.

Engagement and cancellation

- This proposal is valid for acceptance by the Client until [date];
- If accepted, work can commence within three weeks of receipt of first payment / signing of contract, provided that local permits, accommodation and support are arranged;
- The Client may cancel the engagement at any time with a 30-day written notice to the Supplier at..., in Canada. In that case fees until the end of the cancellation period and all expenses become due immediately;
- The Client and Supplier may agree to extend the engagement period;
- If, for unforeseeable reasons, the project needs to be extended beyond the targeted six-month length, the Supplier will commit to make resources available on a best effort basis to ensure successful completion of the project.

It is expected that such an extension would not take longer than an additional two months.

Other

- The Supplier is responsible for deliverables as outlined in the 'Objectives / deliverables', 'Roles / responsibilities' and 'Measuring success' sections of this proposal and for executing the project with the highest professional standards, according to the approach outlined in this proposal, using global best practices as they apply to such engagements (see Attachment 3);
- The Client retains responsibility for all business decisions and, therefore, for the ultimate results of the project. The Supplier assumes no responsibility for any business decisions and their results as they relate to this project or otherwise;
- The Supplier is 3-i Inc. of Toronto, Canada. However, it is understood that Sandy Vaci will be personally engaged for the majority of the project's time (75% or more).

Submitted, on behalf of 3-i Inc., on..., in Toronto: 3-i Inc.:________________	Accepted, on behalf of the Bank, on ..., in__________: (Name:____________________) (Title:____________________)

Case study 10: Detailed implementation guide of best practices

What follows is the 'nitty-gritty' of the proposal reviewed above. The proposal set up a hypothetical situation using consulting help to implement best practices and detailed how to phase the project, how to track success, make decisions about next steps, etc.

This case study adds the detailed outline of what resources are needed in such a situation. It should serve as a useful guide regarding expectations towards consultants offering help. Alternatively, by totalling up the resource requirements on the consulting and company sides, one can get the total requirements fairly easily.

To carry on with the format, everything is presented as it would be in an actual proposal – as attachments to the recommendation and upfront overview.

Attachment 1: Project phases and options – Phases 0 and 1 (including Phase 1 options)

Phase	Scope	Outcome	Consulting support	Time requirement	Fee estimate
0	High level situation, feasibility, cost assessment	Phase 1 proposal, off-site presentation	1.00 FTE	0.75 mo (Completed)	N.A. (gratis)
1A	Global 'best in class' sales processes and management practices / templates (branch / loans focus, personal bankers and BDRs, alternative channels as needed)	4 branches in pilot, local staff ready to implement roll-out, full documentation	1.25 FTE	6 mo	C$[xxx]
1B	As 1A, plus CRM and marketing review / support	CRM recommendation, revised marketing plans, best data cleansing and	1.50 FTE	6 mo (no additional elapsed time, can be executed within same time frame with + 0.25 FTE consulting support)	C$[xxx]
1C	As 1B, plus customer base, product and operational reviews	Best product / customer activity plans for improved profitability	1.75 FTE	Needs discussion, pending talent availability	TBD
1D	As 1C, plus full alternative delivery channel integration review	Best in class alternative channel integration plans	2.00 FTE	Needs discussion, pending talent availability	TBD

Comments / summary

- The proposal is to proceed with Phase 1A to limit costs and ensure feasibility. CRM, marketing and alternative channel issues to be addressed to the extent that they need to be, to ensure the success of Phase 1A;
- Phase 1A fee estimate represents 30% 'long-term engagement discount' versus standard fee schedule for a six-month full engagement of 1.25 FTE. Note that additional consulting fees for extra resources that may be needed to execute the project will be at 3-i Inc.'s cost. Therefore, only their additional and pre-agreed out-of-pocket expenses may be charged to the Bank;

Attachment 1 (continued): Project phases and options – Phase 2 options

Phase	Scope	Outcome	Consulting support	Time requirement	Fee estimate
2A	National roll out of 'sales boost Pilot'	Duplicate results achieved in test, embed new approach across network	0.25 FTE max.	2–6 mo (to be defined during Phase 1)	C$[xxx] max.
2B	As 2A, plus extend coverage to SME and credit card sales force	Duplicate results of loans / personal banking across SME and credit cards	0.75 FTE max.	6 mo max.	C$[xxx] max
2C	As 2B, plus include all alternative sales and service channels	Full integration of all channels for best results	1.50 FTE (est.)	6–9 mo, to be defined later	TBD, depending on time, support needs and talent availability

Comments / summary

- Phase 2 options presented as indicative alternatives only. The proposal is to proceed with Phase 1 (starting with Option A) and evaluate next steps towards the end of the agreed-upon Phase 1 stage(s);
- Note that Phase 2A resource estimate assumes successful completion of Phase 1A. That is, local resources should be able to handle most of the national roll-out implementation based on what they have learned working with the Consultant during Phase 1A, and based on the documentation / templates available from Phase 1A. Therefore, only minimal consulting support (no more than 0.25 FTE) is assumed;
- Phase 2B may also be possible using mostly internal resources, relying on knowledge gained from Phase 1. In an ideal situation consulting fees could be kept to no more than C$[xxx] for the entire Phase 2B execution. This would assume a '20% of time' retainer for six months for consulting services and executing everything internally.

Attachment 2: Bank's resource requirements – Phase 1, Option A

Person / level / functional area	Level of involvement	% of FTE time required	Other
ADMINISTRATIVE / EXECUTIVE			
- Project leader	Full time	100%	Experience in BEP, project management, sales logistics and processes, good at knowledge transfer ('Consultant's local face')
- Admin support	Moderate	10–25%	Meetings, travel logistics, other support
- Head of retail bank	Light	5–10%	Ongoing direction, senior level support
- Executive management	Occasional	2–5%	Monthly review meetings, timely decisions
SALES			
- Sales Planning / Logistics	Medium	25 - 50%	May be lighter, depending project leader's qualifications
- Regional Sales Head(s)	Moderate	10 - 25%	Depends on willingness to participate and get hands on experience upfront
- Branch Managers	Light	5 - 10%	Local input, support and guidance
- Branch Ops / Credit / Quality / Other	Occasional	2 - 5%	To optimise capacity / process planning
MARKETING			
- Head of Marketing	Light	5 - 10%	Depends on availability of database / direct marketing support, assumes Option A only
- Database / Direct marketing manager	Moderate	10 - 25%	May be substituted by IT / MIS support if qualified marketing person is not available
OTHER			
- IT - MIS	Light	5 - 10%	If no system / programming changes
- IT - CRM	Light	5 - 10%	Assumes Option A only, higher involvement with other Options (10–25%)
- HR / Training	Moderate / Medium	10 - 50%	Training programme development and delivery (depends on efficiency / background of resources and level of outsourcing)
- Credit	Light	5 - 10%	Ensure proper targeting for activities
- Operations	Light	5 - 10%	Process alignment across full delivery chain
- Call Centre Manager / Delegate	Light	5 - 10%	Proper activity planning and execution

Comments / summary

- Excluding admin support and the full time local project leader, the 'load' on local resources is between 1.0 and 2.4 FTE for the duration of the project (estimated at six months / 26 weeks for Phase 1, Option A). This corresponds to an average blended requirement of 1.7 FTE functional support (the average blended support requirement is 2.9 FTE including the full time local project leader and admin support);
- These estimates are based on observed level of performance by competent staff in the same positions in other companies and markets. With higher / lower efficiencies these time requirements may decline / increase;
- The above support requirement does not include time required from personal bankers and BDRs in the pilot branches, and from personnel in the customer care centre to do outbound telemarketing. This is because their workload should reflect their rebalanced efforts under the new sales set-up. As such, it is to be part of their future daily activities and not be additional;
- The workload may vary throughout the project – this can be clarified / refined during 'Step 1 / Start Up' of the project if needed;
- Resource allocation from the Consultant 3-i Inc. is estimated at 1.25 FTE for the same duration.

Attachment 3: Sales boost project – Phase 1A building blocks

Block	Duration	Sample activities
Initiation	3 weeks	Select local project leader and support staff Select branches participating in pilot Communicate project and its goals internally Kick off meeting with all project participants Refine project plan and allocate detailed tasks
Foundation	6 weeks	Sales staff capacity assessment in selected branches, define capacity reallocation model to free up time Detailed review of existing sales practices / processes, sales management basics, identify gaps to be bridged Review business vs. sales vs. marketing plans, central vs. branch-level objectives and activity plans Database review per participating branch, establish possible level of information support Define and start immediate implementation of customer information gathering marketing activities as needed (to make up for database gaps in pilot branches) Review central and local sales support tools and marketing materials / processes Branch- and central-level operational process review and identify changes needed if any Input from Credit re. target segment selection for sales actions
Build-up	6 weeks	Assess sales skills, define new training modules needed (e.g. prospect profiling, cross-selling, scripting, objection handling) Develop training modules as needed Define benchmarks, expectations, branch level objective setting approach Identify tracking needs, establish IT feasibility, define optimal solution, start set-up Outline sales management programme, develop templates to be implemented (e.g. meeting schedules, activity planning, performance management, special rewards) Develop consensus on individual performance-related variable compensation Develop and template optimal sales process Define marketing, operational, credit process integration needed to make above successful Review role of alternative delivery channels and define optimal level of integration at this stage

Implementation	6 weeks	Conduct training as needed Implement sales processes and sales management discipline, embed templated approaches, coach as needed Integrate marketing, alternative delivery, operational, credit and other processes for start-up Implement tracking and reward system Template, test, dry run and operationalise integrated set-up
Start-up	2 weeks	Start activities, monitor results, identify weak points to address, unique local problems to fix ('Measuring success; Level B')
Monitor	3 weeks	Confirm efficiency improvements based on early trends ('Measuring success; Level C-1') Outline roll-out plans based on results and lessons learned

Chapter 5
International sales organisations: moving cross-border

A whole new area of opportunities and complications open up when a company decides to go international, into different markets. Yet this is fast becoming the standard in retail banking across the globe. An expert sales practitioner therefore must be familiar with what it takes to operate across borders and expand sales capacities cross-border.

This chapter deals with some of the basics:

- The benefits;
- The set-up models; and
- The main issues – how to identify them and how to address them.

Benefits for the bank

Going international has a multitude of benefits, beyond the purely personal one of being able to move into many more potential sales jobs with exciting opportunities, in exciting new markets:

- For the business as a whole an international base offers more diversification, more stability, more stable revenues, with risks better spread (and, hence, lowered) – meaning higher and more stable income today;
- It also offers new opportunities by being present in new markets – hence higher future revenue potential tomorrow;
- It allows for spreading the cost of central support functions across more business units, economies of scale when negotiating with third parties, transferring knowledge and 'inventing the wheel' only once – in net, lower relative costs today;
- Finally, it gives a company access to a more diverse talent base with background in different settings – resulting in lower cost of ideas tomorrow.

Benefits for the sales function

We have already mentioned the purely personal benefit of having more career opportunities available to the best sales people, in different, exciting markets, with additional experience and earnings potential. Done right, though, there are also institutional benefits for the sales area as a whole.

As knowledge gets transferred across markets local skills improve and time to market with the best ideas (from any market, not just home-grown) decreases.

Negotiating alliance deals, training programmes and many more third-party opportunities that directly affect the sales area become easier as multi-market weight is put behind the negotiating team.

By having a well co-ordinated international sales function, management benefits because it has a faster and better grasp of numbers and trends, as they are immediately passed through the central sales function from local markets.

Costs decline as, for example, sales materials developed somewhere else can be reapplied in other markets, saving development effort (time and cost).

Motivation increases as sales people visiting other countries where the bank is present recognise their own home practices and take pride in being part of a 'uniformly best' company.

Finally, if the 'home country' is at a more advanced stage, 'home practices' can be swiftly exported to new markets, giving an immediate boost to the self-esteem and (through better results) earnings potential of sales staff there.

There are many more benefits that one could identify but hopefully these few will make a strong argument that going cross-border is a good thing to happen to sales staff, which should be embraced wholeheartedly.

Table 5.1 summarises some of the benefits mentioned above, for a clearer picture.

Table 5.1: Benefits of a central sales function

People development
- Including more mobility, career planning, training

Improved skills, discipline, learnings transfer
- Better local sales efficiencies, lower acquisition and other costs
- Faster time to market with best ideas

Better negotiating position with outside partners
- Multi-market scale with vendors and alliance partners

Better understanding and control at HO level
- Transparency in plans, level of local development, trends and their causes

Possibility of uniform approach / positioning
- Immediate savings by transfering communication materials, templates
- Long term brand value to organization with "standard image and approach"

Higher support from HO if "home market" is at more evolved stage
- Avoid reinventing the wheel, export what already works and can be applied

Source: 3-i Inc.

International set-ups

To realise all of the above benefits the bank needs to set up the organisation across borders correctly and needs to keep in mind the many pitfalls that await unsuspecting new players in foreign markets.

There are two general models for international organisational set-ups:

- Segment reporting structures; and
- Geographic reporting structures.

Segment reporting

In a pure segment reporting structure, heads of segment-focused business units (for example, head of retail for a country) would not report to the local CEO but would report through to the regional retail executive, who would report to the global retail head, himself being a direct report of the global board or CEO.

The global or regional retail head in this structure would normally also have central support functions, but the country retail head would not report to the person in charge of central activities. However, the key functions, be they profit centres or functional support areas, would normally have dotted-line reporting to the central managers in charge of those areas. This ensures central co-ordination and uniformity across the international group, while keeping bottom line responsibility with local management.

The benefits of this set up are:

- Clear separation of business lines (e.g. retail versus corporate banking), resulting in focused attention and better resources directed at each;
- Higher efficiencies through stronger central coordination.

A schematic representation of this set-up is shown in Figure 5.1.

Figure 5.1: Segment reporting structure

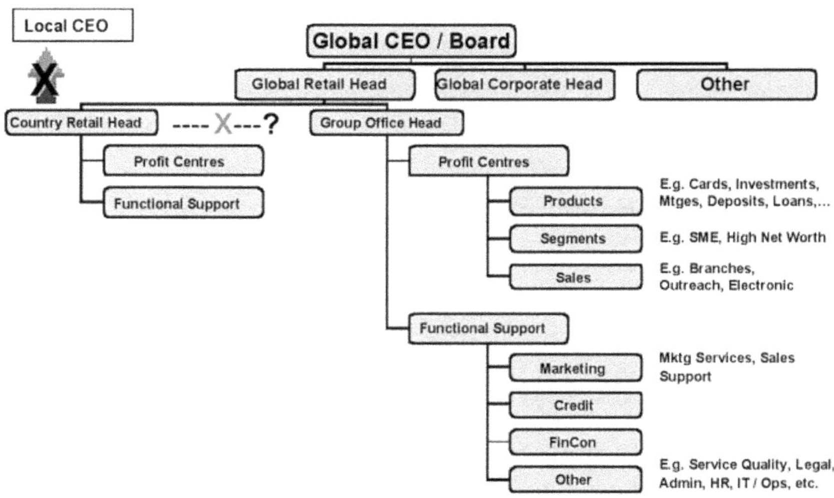

Source: 3-i Inc.

This structure was pioneered by Citibank and its early set-up for its global consumer bank followed the format (see Figure 5.2). However, as with most structures, there is no ultimate right or wrong set-up and they do evolve over time. As a result, Citibank's current structure for its international retail banking organisation looks significantly different, with several exceptions to their own, earlier, rules.

Figure 5.2: Early Citi set-up

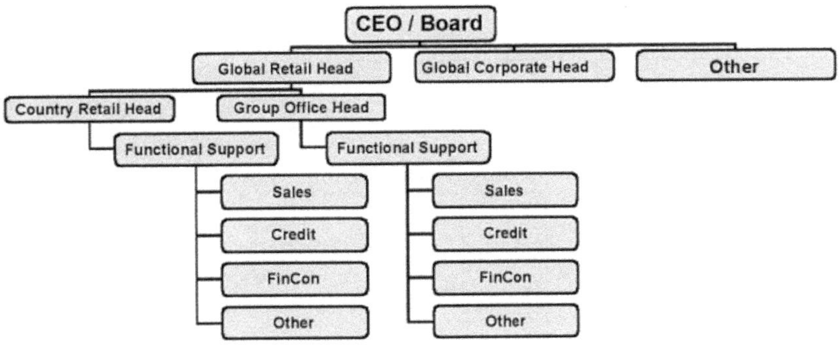

Source: 3-i Inc.

Geographic reporting

At the opposite end of the spectrum is the geographic reporting structure, used initially by GE Finance. It pulls responsibilities together not along segmental (e.g. retail versus corporate) lines, but along geographic lines (e.g. country A versus country B). Local retail heads report to local CEOs, who then report through to head office on a geographical basis. This structure also allows for dotted-line reporting. For example, in many cases local business unit heads report dotted-line to regional / global heads of the same area.

Figure 5.3 illustrates this set-up.

Figure 5.3: Geographic reporting structure

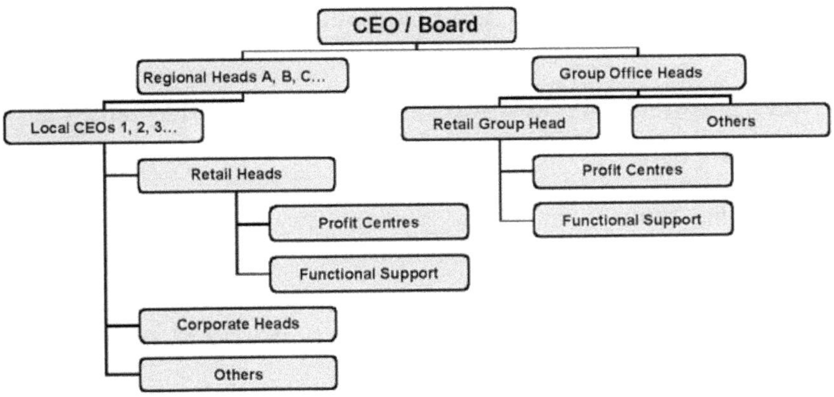

Source: 3-i Inc.

In the case of GE, central support teams are usually set up to help local functional areas either as requested by local management or, more often, as mandated by HQ when financial results do not meet expectations and fixes need to be applied (see Figure 5.4).

Figure 5.4: Early GE Finance set-up

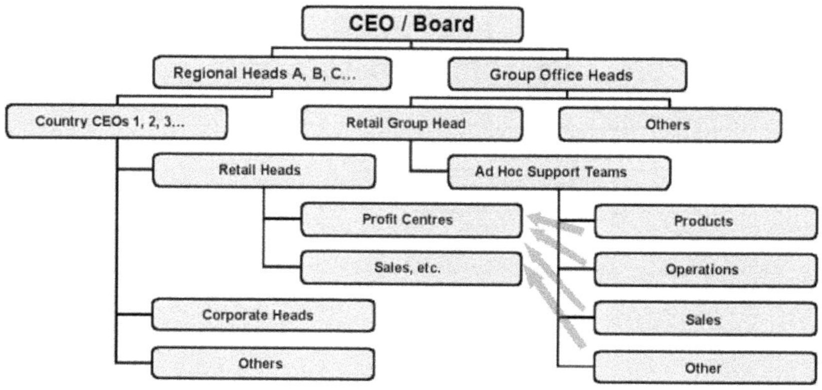

(Where [arrow] shows support provided as *mandated* by HO, or requested by the subsidiary)

Source: 3-i Inc.

Again, GE's structure keeps evolving and their current set-up still seems to be in a flux. In that way it is very similar to Citibank, which started at the opposite end of the spectrum in its approach.

Matrix structures

Whether the basic structure follows a segment or geographical reporting set-up, the common theme in both is that they have dotted-line reporting lines. In other words, they both have 'matrix structures'. Matrix structures try to address the issue of strong local ownership (geographic set-up) versus most efficient global approach (segment set-up).

Matrix structures, however, carry their own issues, as summarised in Table 5.2.

Table 5.2: Key matrix issues

Organisational Alignment

– Head Office and Subsidiary set ups must match, including reporting

Sequence of Evolution

– Functional Support should be established before Central Profit Centres, especially in geographic reporting structures

Organisational Willingness

– Subsidiaries must see value of central functions

– HO must be willing to change organisational set up maximum efficiency with new design

– sales management

– sales processes

Nothing is Static

– Even globally best companies keep evolving and changing structure to fit changing needs; there is no 'given' best structure

Source: 3-i Inc.

Matrix sales structures

Within the overall structure, a matrixed sales set-up must balance central co-ordination and expert input with keeping most accountabilities local. The central function must act as a centre of competence, but the local units must keep local profit and loss (P&L) responsibility.

Roles and responsibilities must clearly be defined and delineated. The central function should have a 'guide, support, control' responsibility, while local management should keep ownership of the agreed sales plans and their execution.

'Guide, support, control' responsibilities include strategic guidance (e.g. agreeing on yearly sales plans), expert support (e.g. training, process design, sales support materials), control of key elements to ensure uniform discipline (e.g. standard sales plans and processes), plus central representation and a responsibility for mentoring individuals and building the organisation across borders.

Central representation can mean either managing cross-border projects and representing the bank to the outside world, or taking over the championing of local plans at head office level once agreed by the central sales function.

Mentoring and building the organisation should be self-explanatory. However, let us keep in mind that moving into a new market frequently means expanding into a less developed area, where local sales experts may have great difficulty in finding anyone to ask questions of. It is up to the central sales function to act as a mentor and supplier of expert knowledge as needed in those cases. The key central and local sales roles are shown in Table 5.3.

Table 5.3: Sales – key roles

Central: 'Guide, Support, Control' – Expert support – Learning transfer – Cross-border, multi-market projects – Central representation of Local Sales • internally at Head Office level • externally in multi-market deals/projects – Build the base: organisation, knowledge
Local: 'Ownership, Knowledge, Entrepreneurship' – Develop, owns and executes Sales Plans

Source: 3-i Inc.

A more detailed overview of the 'guide, support, control' principle is shown in Table 5.4. It details the interaction model between central and local sales, for optimal efficiency. While it may seem that we have spent a lot of time defining the organisational set-up from different angles, this is very essential. More companies fail when going international because they did not set up the organisational structure right than for any other reason. On the other hand, once the structure is defined well, results seem to follow as if by magic…

Table 5.4: Central sales – interaction with local sales

Guide	- sales strategy - business plans - processes, management practices
Support	- all functional areas (training, local marketing, etc.) - all segments and products - mentoring, people development
Control	- sales plans - senior sales staff selection - alliances

Source: 3-i Inc.

A sample of a matrixed sales organisation is also provided in Figure 5.5.

Figure 5.5: Sample matrixed sales organisation

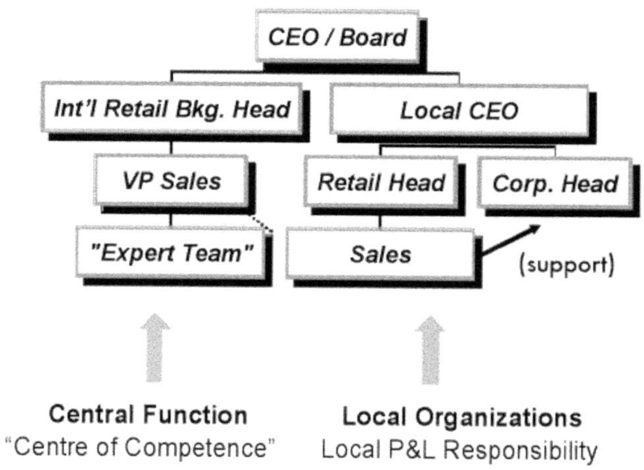

Source: 3-i Inc.

Changing the structure

Setting up the right structure upfront is always easier than reworking something already set up in a sub-optimal way. The help the reader with the latter, more difficult, task, Table 5.5 summarises a well thought out approach to review and rework an already existing international sales structure, to comply with the best matrixed sales set-up guidelines. They are from my own experience, with a major global bank. As such, I can vouch for their effectiveness!

Table 5.5: Four-step international sales structure review

Step 1 – Head Office Review • Review Marketing and the Bank's International set up, issues, expectations; agree on key markets to visit • Understand Executive level commitment to organisational changes that may be needed to implement the most efficient structure • Time required: 2 - 3 days. Elapsed time depends on availability of key Managers ***Step 2 – Key Markets Review*** • Visit 8 – 10 key international markets, talk with Sales Heads and Retail Heads (and CEOs if needed) • Understand: – Level of skills, talents, tools, planning discipline (using standardised templates) – Organisational set up, clarity on existing roles / responsibilities – Key issues from a business and sales perspective, needed support – Organisational readiness to accept central support (and stronger coordination) • Time required: 2 full days per market plus travel. Elapsed time depends on logistics – may take 2 months to fully accomplish ***Step 3 – Situational Assessment*** • Develop scorecard assessment along the 4 dimensions of "understand" step 2 • Compare situations to global best practices and other models as applicable • High level outline best model to evolve to, identify potential issues, benefits, costs for evolving towards it • Time required: 4 – 6 days ***Step 4 – Propose Way Forward*** • Identify areas for improvement and areas to address first, in order to gain early buy in from the markets • First steps for learning transfer and building a 'sales community' • Set expectations in terms of skills, discipline, improvements • Define roles / responsibilities for central and local sales functions, interaction model, reporting, accountabilities • Present, incorporate input, gain approval • Time required: 6 – 8 days. Elapsed time depends on availability of Bank's Management

Source: 3-i Inc.

Some issues (and how to address them)

Having reviewed the benefits of going international and how to set up the organisation for it, the picture would not be complete if we ignored some of the obvious (and not so obvious) issues that go along with such a move. There will be a dozen of them presented in the following section to raise awareness. Where proven techniques exist to address them these will be detailed as well. Where the point is more to make the reader aware that an issue may simply exist, we will stay with simply highlighting it and let it stay at that. Here we go...

The speed of change may differ in a new market

Bankers and sales people used to a certain steady change in fully developed markets may be surprised how fast things change in the emerging world. For illustration, look at Figure 5.6, showing how fast markets can change (e.g. contract) in newly developing markets.

Figure 5.6: Speed of market contraction in CEE

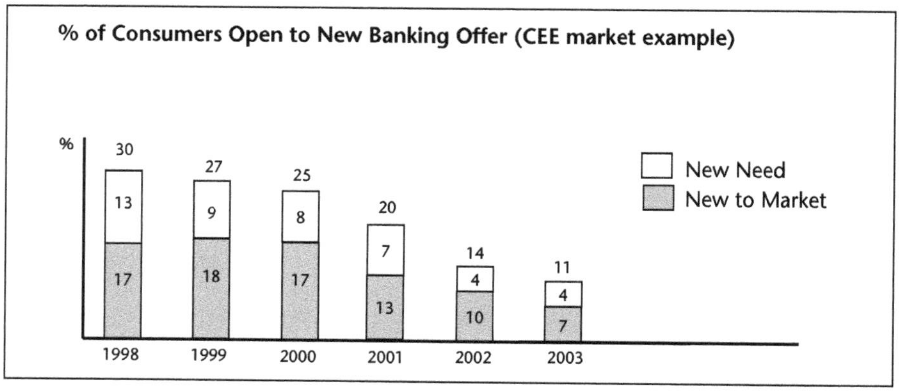

Source: 3-i Inc.

In the same region (Central and Eastern Europe) but in another market, the acceptance of phone banking went from 20% to 65% in just 6 months...

Clearly, being unprepared for such a change can be disastrous for new entrants. Everything needs to be able to change very fast – sales plans, channel plans (such as setting up telephone banking at a moment's notice), strategies (e.g. quickly shifting from targeting the unbanked to targeting the newly banked, based on Figure 5.6) and more.

Information taken for granted in the home market may not be available

This can make sales targeting difficult, if not impossible. Fortunately, one can often overcome this issue by using proxy (substitute) information for what is not available. A good example of using a proxy would be that of Citibank in Poland.

When Citi wanted to expand its target segment for personal loans to professionals, the issue of 'black/grey money' came up. These were cash payments given for services, so taxes would not have to be paid on them.

Try as it might, Citi could not turn the whole local taxation system into a model of transparency overnight. It clearly needed to be able to target people who may not have proven incomes to qualify for loans. This is where common sense came in. For example, any physician who has run their own practice for more than a year successfully and has no outstanding claims against them can be expected to be making good money and have a business model to survive. This is despite tax returns showing zero income and being in constant poverty.

So it would make sense to offer these professionals loans based on their estimated income, which was well known but never officially admitted. By doing so, Citi opened up a very lucrative new segment for their credit offers, which was closed to other banks.

People may not understand your offer

Imagine selling fluoride toothpaste to people in a remote jungle who have never brushed their teeth. You cannot boast about the cavity-fighting properties of your product because they do not know what cavities are. You cannot even sell them the toothpaste on its own because they do not even know what toothpaste is for. You first have to tell them about brushing their teeth, then about doing it with toothpaste, then about why yours is the best toothpaste.

This is similar to the dilemma faced by many banks trying to sell, for example, credit cards in parts of the world where the concept of credit cards itself is not yet understood. Or selling basic banking services to unbanked populations that are not yet familiar with the concept of 'banking'. This is sometimes euphemistically called 'marketing (or selling) in an unprepared environment'.

Luckily, the issue has been faced by a number of banks before and one can rely on their experience to draw up a list of key steps on how to approach such an environment. Figure 5.7 summarises the key differences between selling / marketing in ready versus unready markets.

Figure 5.7: Selling in an 'unprepared environment'

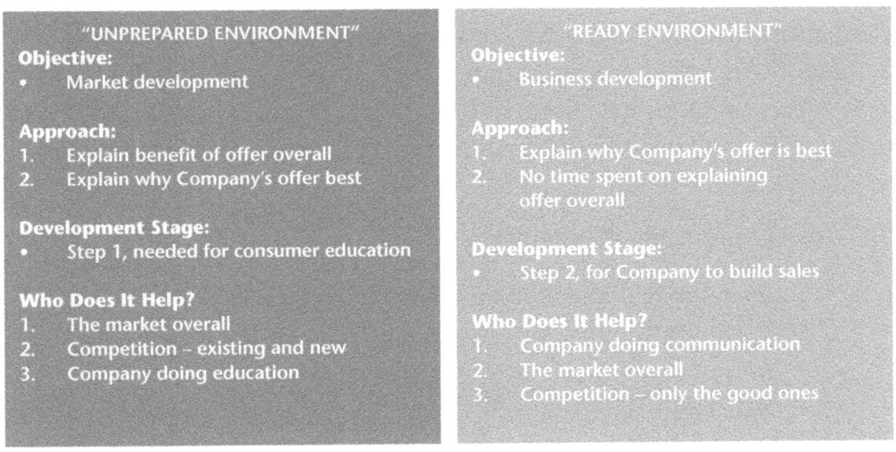

Source: 3-i Inc.

Your basic sales tools may not be available

Direct marketing lists, geodemographic segmentation and many more tools used for proactive business development may not be available in all markets. Basing your sales development plans on them would thus lead to failure. We talked before about how to overcome a lack of basic segmentation data with proxying. However, even some of the more sophisticated tools such as geodemographic segmentation can be 'near-duplicated' with some ingenuity and hard work.

Geodemographic segmentation is based on the principle that people of similar means and tastes tend to congregate together, as in "tell me where you live and I'll tell you who you are". Armed with this information one can target different neighbourhoods with different sales offers and increase their acceptance. However, while geocoding may be available in markets such as the UK, Germany or Belgium, it is not so in many other countries.

The solution? Nothing substitutes for getting out of the branch and walking around the neighbourhood. I have met a branch manager with a most sophisticated geocoding model to guide his sales people in a country where such information was not at all available. When I asked her how she did it, she simply said: "I walked around the neighbourhoods and wrote down what the best streets and addresses are and all my other observations. It took me three hours every day for two weeks but I got a database out of it that none of my competitors have. And we made good use of it too!"

I will let you draw your own conclusions…

Cover the downside well (better than at home)

Tax avoidance and corruption may play a much bigger role in many newly evolved markets than in more established ones. We have already seen examples of addressing some of these issues (Citibank in Poland, mentioned earlier) in the consumer banking area. Issues get more difficult to deal with in the SME domain. Let us again look at CEE for some examples. Note that this region is not the 'worst case', but in fact half-way between standard markets and undeveloped ones.

Yet the number of SME enterprises that are set up solely to avoid taxes is more than twice that of Western Europe and almost three times as high as in the US and Canada (see Figure 5.8). One can imagine the difficulty banks and their sales forces have in assessing the real needs of these companies and deciding which ones to target!

Figure 5.8: SMEs in CEE – tax avoidance issues

1. High number of SMEs set up only to avoid taxes: up to **80 %**
2. Large "grey economy":

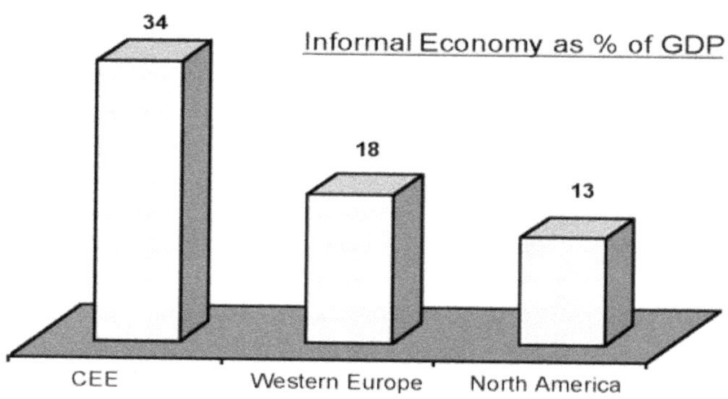

Source: World Bank, 3-i Inc.

To make things even more interesting, corruption is still perceived as part of doing business in CEE (see Figure 5.9). The implication for banks is many-fold.

Obviously, business owners may not be used to straight dealing, not even with banks. This creates additional issues as they may try to haggle over details which cannot be negotiated by sales people. Owners may also take certain practices for granted that could endanger their businesses. Those companies should obviously not be included in target segments. But how to identify them?

Figure 5.9: SMEs in CEE – business opacity issues

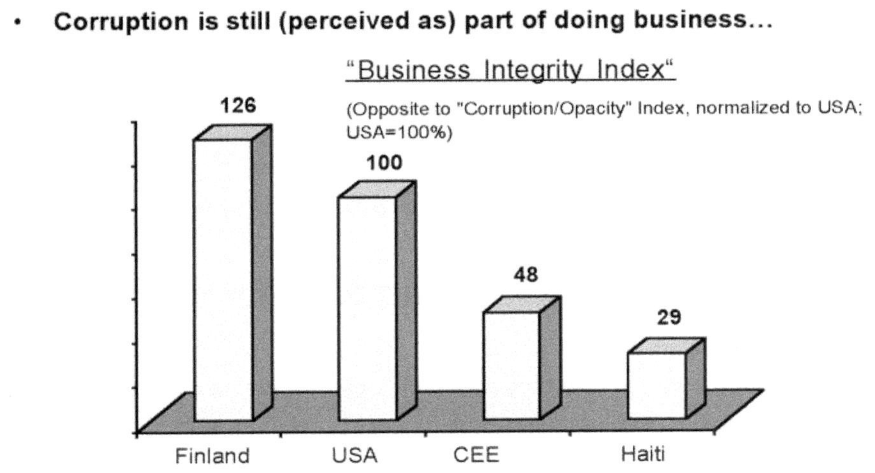

Source: The Economist, 3-i Inc.

Be ready to simplify, supplement or supply processes

Again, all markets are not created equal. But this does not mean that we have to shy away from trying to design the most appropriate processes, for the given market(s).

We may need to *simplify* processes. If electronic data transfer is not available, maybe faxes will do. International banks used this way of sending referrals between sales units in India, for example, when ramping up consumer banking operations there 5–10 years ago. Those who waited for the 'right' IT infrastructure to be put in place were left behind as the 'less sophisticated' but more nimble, smarter competition stole their target customers.

Some banks also showed ingenuity in lesser developed areas of the Far East. Faced with an inefficient postal system they set up their own mail delivery service to allow them to sell credit cards. This is a good example of *supplementing* existing processes, even when they fall outside the Bank's area.

There are also many examples of *supplying* new processes to enable banks to carry out sales with maximum efficiency. I hope, however, that the reader will bear with me as I illustrate creativity in this area not with banking examples, but with an example of how even a government institution (the post office) in an underdeveloped country (Albania) can create the most efficient process by taking advantage of local peculiarities. Surely, if they can do it banks can too...

One sees many children running around frantically in the streets of Tirana, the Albanian capital, carrying big bags. As it turns out, they are 'mail delivery employees' of the Post Office. Due to several street name changes, lack of funds to change street signs and people being used to addressing letters in very descriptive ways, mail delivery relying on correct addresses is near impossible in Tirana. Letters, for example, may be addressed as "in that house behind such-and-such a statue in this park". Delivering them through standard means would be prohibitively expensive.

At the same time, there are many street kids who know their neighbourhoods very well, have free time and would like to make some money. An idea was born. The Post Office reinvented its mail delivery processes. It hired street kids to deliver mail in their neighbourhoods with those 'descriptive' addresses. It offered them a small compensation for this. It put a control mechanism in place, checking randomly if mail had indeed been delivered as claimed by these unusual new employees. The net result was faster delivery, cheaper and more reliable.

Financial services regulations could be different

Of course, if another country has more restrictive regulations, for example on licensing sales people, they need to be followed. However, it is also a good idea to review regulations in all the markets where the bank is present and try to comply with the more advanced ones, even in less regulatorily advanced jurisdictions. For example, giving thorough training to sales people selling mortgages or investments would make sense even if not required locally. It will also result in a sales / service quality advantage over lazier competitors.

Target segments may be different

While consumer needs tend to be similar across different markets, the way people satisfy them may differ. And their means to satisfy their needs may also change dramatically from one market to another. Western Europe, with its social safety net and pension schemes presents very different prospects for its elderly populations compared with the US or some other parts of the world. Indeed, simply projecting target segments from, say, Austria to Hungary could be disastrous, and this is despite a good deal of shared history, physical proximity, similar size and open borders.

The population aged 60+ in Austria is very well off, as they lived through boom times and are well taken care of by their companies and the government. The same population in Hungary is the most destitute, as they have lived through years of communism which did not allow them to accumulate assets, then their government-mandated pensions inflated away as communism fell and market forces kicked in. Targeting the 60+ population with investments and offers related to vacation properties makes sense in Austria but not at all in Hungary.

People define financial terms differently

Calling a debit card a credit card, or thinking of investments as speculation based on inside information are just two examples of what I encountered when opening banking operations in different countries. Sales people need to clearly understand what is what and how their target customers think about them. The sales support area needs to take all of this into account when developing materials. Sales training needs to account for it. The list goes on...

Different overall regulatory frameworks drive different customer attitudes

There are certain embedded customer attitudes which are difficult to change, try as one might. In many markets people are not comfortable with using credit. In some other countries there is no history of borrowing to buy a house. Even in some of the most advanced markets (think of Germany) people may not feel comfortable with 'investments' unless both capital and return are guaranteed – leaving us with fixed term deposits and savings accounts as the investment portfolio we can recommend.

It is essential that these differences are understood by sales management and are tracked by the bank. If consumers want guaranteed capital and return, can we offer them capital guaranteed bonds with minimum guaranteed returns, to serve as investments with 'training wheels'? If credit is a dirty word, should we pitch credit cards purely on convenience and evolve people's spending patterns later? The answer to both questions is a definite yes.

In terms of tracking changes, the evolution of mortgage markets is a good example. In many countries people had not been used to borrowing to buy a home. Governments slowly realised that home ownership is desirable and started to offer incentives to that effect. This resulted in exponential growth in many previously underdeveloped mortgage markets, as government subsidies and tax cuts were heavily advertised. Those banks that caught the trend first and had pre-selected target lists to go after with sales proposals reaped most of the benefits of this growth.

Delivery channels develop at a different pace

A cardinal mistake that many banks make is assuming that the channel structure in new markets should be similar to the home market's. Yet, even in some of the most underdeveloped European markets mobile phone banking ('GSM banking') may be much more developed than in the highly evolved North American markets.

On the other hand, internet usage may be woefully low compared to the US. Any American bank attempting to export its sales structure with a North American channel set-up (strong on internet banking, weak on mobile phone offers) will under-perform in Europe (where the opposite is true, except in Scandinavia).

Customers react differently to promotions and other offers

This is a truism but needs repeating. The proof: I have heard a sales manager at a major international bank, newly transferred from Turkey to Belgium, remarking how undeveloped Belgium's ATM system was because it did not offer US dollar withdrawals. What did not occur to her, even after a year of living in the country, is that US dollar withdrawals offer no benefit to customers in Belgium, as opposed to Turkey which at that point was struggling with hyper-inflation.

And, talking about promotional offers, giving away a free gun with a term deposit in the US must look as shocking to someone from Hong Kong as the Hong Kong offer of gambling with your rate of return on a similar deposit must seem to someone from the US.

I hope the above list of key issues will help any practitioner to avoid them and allow practitioners to handle sales set-ups and processes with the greatest possible efficiency as their bank moves across borders.

www.ingramcontent.com/pod-product-compliance
Ingram Content Group UK Ltd.
Pitfield, Milton Keynes, MK11 3LW, UK
UKHW052301280926
15471UKWH00006B/1053

9 781907 720031